The Mirror of Inner Beauty

illuminating the essence of your soul

ANGELA JONES-TAUL

The Mirror of Inner Beauty

Copyright © 2020 Angela Jones-Taul

All rights reserved. Published in the United States of America.
No part of this book may be reproduced or transmitted in
any form or by any means, graphic, electronic, or mechanical,
including photocopying, recording, taping or by any
information storage or retrieval system, without the permission
in writing from the publisher.

Printed in the USA

ISBN-13: 978-1-949001-75-4 print edition
ISBN-13: 978-1-949001-76-1 ebook edition

Cover design by Candy Lyn Thomen - Seraphim Art of Soul

Published by DreamSculpt Books and Media

An imprint of:

Waterside Productions
2055 Oxford Ave
Cardiff, CA.92007

dedication

This book is dedicated to my mom, aunts, daughter, and granddaughter. To the women placed in my path that showed me strength, compassion, and inspiration. To the women that will become inspired by my journey to share their stories. To God for being the one constant in my life and never failing me. To myself, you're an amazing woman never forget who you are

ACKNOWLEDGMENTS

I want to thank Jared Rosen and Lynn Kitchen for granting me this amazing opportunity to tell my story. Winning the writing contest from Dreamsculpt was a dream come true. I'm forever grateful for the support and encouragement.

To Gloria Coppola my mentor, coach and friend. Thank you for never giving up on me. Your guidance and insight helped me stay on course when I often wanted to give up. I owe you much gratitude and love. I hope you are proud of me.

My cheerleaders thank you for making a girl feel special. Your words of encouragement meant the world to me. Small town love is better than big city lights any day in my book.

TABLE OF CONTENTS

Foreword ix
Introduction xi

Chapter 1: Mirror of Shame; Self-Judgment 1
Chapter 2: The Dark Mask; Self-Hatred 27
Chapter 3: Peeling Away the Mask; Self-Respect 44
Chapter 4: This is Me; Self-Acceptance 62
Chapter 5: I'm Alive; Self-Care 74
Chapter 6: Own Your Beauty; Self-Esteem 83
Chapter 7: Mirror of Inner Beauty; Self-Love 92

Goddess Mode 103
Steps for Finding Your Inner Goddess 113

FOREWORD

The Mirror of Inner Beauty: Illuminating the Essence of Your Soul

It takes a lot of courage to put yourself out there to be judged by others. It's like playing show and tell. Angela lets you into her world where you should feel privileged to be. Get the tissues because you will be sad at times, but you will also see a woman grow from her struggles. This book is an inspiration to all women. We all go through things and it may take years but if you put forth the effort like Angela has you will thrive. She pushed. She endured. She survived. She is an inspiration.

T.M. Shivener Author of Ginger Devil

INTRODUCTION

My soul became wounded early in life, and over the years I lost my own identity while trying to live up to the approval of society. The mirror became an enemy. The reflection I saw showed all my faults. A constant reminder of what hurt me and what I struggled to release. As my pain increased, a mask developed for me to hide behind.

Growing up, I had no understanding of how important self-love was or even how to achieve this crucial tool to keep my sanity. The search for love and acceptance kept me looking in all the wrong places, instead of within myself, making me a target for manipulative behaviors from others. Expecting and accepting less than what I deserved. A people-pleasing, codependent, sensitive empath who had no idea that her happiness couldn't be found in others.

Instead of me balancing out, I was lost without a clue of how to find my way. Wandering in the darkness and my light, at times, got dimmer to the point it was almost gone. I'm declaring now, and with the help of writing this book, that I am the one to make the change for myself. No one else can do this except me. This is my time and place; the past no longer defines me. I live in the "Presence of Now." My trials and tribulations are not for dwelling upon; they are to build and strengthen. Growth and maturity have fueled a passion for living my best life. A goddess arising and emerging into her purpose. Letting go of past hurts and the victim mentality. Stepping out of limiting beliefs to pursue my dreams. My soul is being called to spread an awareness that you can be happy and experience life on a higher vibration. My story is one that most people can relate to and find where they may be holding on to emotional baggage that weighs them down. Character flaws you wish to hide. Unhealthy coping mechanisms that seem to only make matters worse.

My desires for you as the reader are to be inspired, face your own mirror, and discard the mask that may be holding you back from your inner beauty. Letting your light shine through and expressing yourself in a creative way that makes your soul happy. Finding closure and peace in leaving your past hurts behind. Exploring your inner desires and dreams that may take you places you thought only the lucky people get to experience.

We all fall short at times, but the goal is not to stay there in condemnation but to forgive and be forgiven. Your purpose on this earth is different from mine; we are all here for a reason. Let yourself be open to a newfound freedom that comes from being and honoring who you are.

The mirror can be scary and hard to face, but once you recognize the beauty that comes from within, the outer shell can't compete anymore. For you have found the key to unlocking false beliefs that come from shame, guilt, social conditioning, and any trauma. All it takes is the courage to believe in who you are meant to be.

The Mirror of Inner Beauty

Mirror, mirror on the wall
I'm not sure why I fear you most of all.
What I see is three stages of me
The little girl, the passive women, and the goddess within.
How do I get them all to agree?
Can't there only be one queen?
Patience and tenacity will be our guide
To help navigate our bumpy ride.
Oh, mirror don't be sad.
For one day I will see
The mirror of inner beauty illuminating my soul.
Then the three will once see their reflection is all of me.

Angela Jones-Taul

***A Goddess**
**Is a woman who emerges from deep within
herself. She is a woman who has honestly
explored her darkness and learned to celebrate
her light. She is a woman who knows of the
magic and mysterious places inside her, the
sacred places that can nurture her soul and
make her whole. She is a woman who radiates
light. She is magnetic. -Unknown*

1
MIRROR OF SHAME

Mirror, mirror on the wall, early in life you were my downfall, only seeing what I judged to be my flaw, like an open sore I felt raw.

I'd like to think that a few moments before my mother gave her last big push for me to be born, an angel whispered to my soul. "Embrace your light at all times, even in your darkest moments, you will be a healer, nurturer and a voice; your natural essence will always ignite the inner beauty." On May 4, 1972, I was born into this world equipped with love, confidence, strength, and beauty.

Less than a month before my second birthday, a heart attack would take the life of my father. My parents had separated before I was born, and now the opportunity to have a relationship with him was gone. My age kept me from understanding what death meant. Explaining this is hard because I have no memory of the actual event. The emotional energy that surrounded me from my two older brothers and mom made an impact on me. I felt the grief, and it left me restless. Being this young, I didn't know how to express what I was feeling. Maybe I cried or wouldn't stay asleep. I'm unsure of how it all played out, but I knew something was missing.

Taking your first step as a child is terrifying yet exciting. As you hold on to a loved one's hand for security, they slowly start to let go, and you take two small steps by yourself. Then you get braver and start taking steps without help. Soon no one can keep up with the busy toddler. How I wish my experience with walking were this textbook. Astigmatism, the medical term for blurry vision, was my problem. I kept running into walls and doors, and my mom knew this was not normal. This would mean I would have to wear glasses. My memory for recalling the exact experience of seeing things clearer for the first time fails me, but I imagine it went as follows: I was sitting on my mother's lap as the doctor placed these tiny black-rimmed glasses on me. Smiling wholeheartedly as a crisp, clear, vivid picture of my surroundings appeared. Turning my head to see the defining features of my mother's face, then looking at the doctor and everything around me. What an amazing discovery for me. Everything was bold and in focus, no more squinting. They were the cutest pair of glasses for such a small face. Having to wear glasses didn't matter because I needed them, seeing better made me happy. I really wish mom would have kept the glasses for me. They could have reminded me that clarity comes with the right tools.

After a few years, my sister was born. It was nice having a sister around. She was a brat, but we managed to get along. Her dad lived with us, and I considered us a family, so when our parents married, it was just a formality. He never once made me feel like I wasn't his own flesh and blood. He treated us all like his own. I didn't have that father-daughter bond that comes from having the initial contact after birth. But what he did give me was the closest form of having a dad I would ever experience.

Many memories flood my mind as I think back to how my childhood experiences made me feel very different. My sister, cousins, and friends all had a pretty decent length of hair. I, on the other hand, had peach fuzz. My ponytails were so short and stingy. I have no idea how my mom was able to put those antlers on my head. This would be the beginning of not feeling comfortable with how I looked. When we moved to "on the hill," it put us in a different school district. The city school kids were mostly black and often teased us about being in a predominantly white school. I was probably affected by it more than my brothers. When we would go to church on Sundays and choir practices, I had to hear all the bad-mouthing. I would listen to some of the girls talking about how I was a goody two-shoes, or that I was the favorite. In defense, I would say nothing; just sit there and allow them to talk, but secretly I wanted to run and hide. I just wanted to do my best in everything, not to make them dislike me. Battling the need to feel accepted, when all I was doing was trying to be me. This would begin my feeling that I wasn't good enough or worthy because I was always being talked about. In school I was never approached with any racial inequalities because I was black. Most of my friends were white, and to me, there was no color barrier; we were all the same. I really didn't have to try hard to have friends. I was one of those likable people. The need to feel like I belonged was my hidden hurt that wasn't easy to talk about. How do I tell everyone the girl who seems to have it all together feels completely broken?

At home, some tension was building with my mom and stepdad. He took my sister and me out to eat one afternoon. He wanted to talk about mom and him getting a divorce. We were both still young, around the ages of six and ten. A lump began to form in my throat, my heart felt heavy, and I began to cry. He comforted us and reassured us that everything would be all right. For me, I was losing a dad again, feeling helpless in a situation I had no control over. Did anyone understand that I was beginning to become an emotional wreck?

Being allowed to go with my sister for visits and overnight stays helped with my pain, but it made me curious about my real dad. My brothers had some letters from our dad that were written when he and mom separated. I can vaguely remember one of the letters my brother let me read that had my name mentioned. He asked how I was doing and stated for my brothers to watch out for me. My dad had four other children besides my brothers and me. We all know each other and have an amazing bond. Our mothers weren't caught up in what we today call "baby mama drama." In total, my father has seven children. That didn't matter to me, I just wanted to know him. Sensitive, quiet, and meek were the core qualities of my personality while growing up. Adapting to each situation to the best of my ability for my age.

Mom purchased a HUD house a few years after her divorce. We moved on a cold winter day in January. 2278 Mefford Fort Dr. was the new address. A small three-bedroom, one-bath brick house at the end of a cul-de-sac. It had a big backyard with plenty of room to play, black shutters around the windows, and concrete steps leading up to the house. Everyone always wanted to hang out at our house. Not sure why, I guess they just felt welcomed, ate good food, and had a loving respect for my mother. My brothers always had friends over from the basketball and football teams. We were all a big family. It was nice hanging out when they let me. Most of the time they would just kick me out of the living room.

I was about 12 years old when I started receiving some attention from an older man who would frequently visit our home. He was a black man about 20 years old, good-looking, stocky build, around 5' 8", hair cut close. When he would come around, it would make me nervous and feel giddy inside. At first, he would just wink at me and make a point to say something to make me smile. He told me I could be his secret girlfriend. Receiving this type of attention was new to me, I wasn't sure how to respond. Remembering the exact details of how we ended up at the house alone is a blur. It was not unusual for me to be home for 30 minutes to an hour by myself after school on certain days. Mom worked full time, and my brothers would come straight home after their practices. My sister could have been at a relative's house. When I heard the knock at the door, I was a little startled because I wasn't expecting anyone. Looking out the window, I saw him standing on the small porch. Not fearing to let him inside, I opened the door. "They aren't home yet," is what I stated as I was holding open the screen door. "I know, sweetness. I'm here to see you," was his reply. A warm sensation formed on my cheeks, and I smiled. Inviting him in didn't seem like a bad thing, he came over all the time. He asked me to come sit down next to him on the couch. I still remember the light tan couch, with dark and light brown specs in the design. He patted the couch cushion for me to come sit next to him. The smell of his cologne – a musky, manly scent – tickled my nose. Very gently, he took my hand, placing it on his penis. I froze! Nervous energy began to build. Next, he was unzipping his pants and exposed himself to me. Flashes of after-school specials about girls being rape entered my mind. Slowly he started to push my head to go down on him, giving me instructions on how to give him pleasure. What happens if I vomit on him? Are my teeth supposed to touch it? Why is he having me do this? Questions I never asked because of being too scared. Groping my breast and putting his hands down my pants to touch my genitals. This is where I get confused about feelings because my body started reacting to his touch, and it felt good. He told me to go down faster on him until he finally ejaculated in my mouth. Immediately I got up and ran to the bathroom to clean up. Hurrying to get myself back to normal and change my clothes before my brothers got home. In my room I sat on the bed, trying to keep tears from falling. On his way back from cleaning himself up, he reminded me not to tell anyone and that I had done a great job.

A feeling of guilt and shame overcame me immediately. This was wrong, and I was going to be in a lot of trouble. A few minutes later I heard my brothers come in; he lied and told them he had just pulled up before them. Peeking their heads in to my room to check on me, I told them I wasn't feeling good. They reassured me mom would be home soon. After this incident, anytime my friends could have me ride the bus home with them, I was begging my mom for permission to let me. Sometimes I wasn't that lucky, and the abuse would happen again.

We never had intercourse. He only had me perform oral sex and he would touch me. I was scared to tell anyone because I didn't think they would believe me. Punishment and a scolding were what I feared from my mom. Sugarcoating the truth gave me the courage to tell her finally. Explaining he was bothering me to do stuff, not that I had already done them. The abuse and him coming over stopped after that. Several years later I found out that my mom had threatened his life if he ever came near me again.

My core beauty of who I was had been disrupted. What reason could explain a grown man approaching me in this way? Damaged goods was how I saw myself. I built a wall, one that would eventually imprison my soul.

Although the abuse had stopped, I still had guys that would approach me. I felt like everyone knew my secret and I was a target. Oral sex was popular because it was an easy way to get a guy off, and you didn't have to worry about getting pregnant. They would tell me what other girls were doing for them, and my insecurities began to surface. Desperate for attention, and not understanding this was negative, I often gave in to their demands.

Intercourse would become the next step I would feel pressured to perform. Having a boyfriend was nice and made me feel secure. This alleviated the need to allow others to pressure me. Unfortunately, he would want us to go all the way, but I was scared to have sex. Doing the other stuff was nothing because I had learned to make myself feel numb from the abuse but allowing someone to penetrate me was frightening. We tried, but it didn't happen. I was way too nervous. So, he broke up with me, typical teenage boy stuff. One of the guys who I had done favors for talked me into letting him go all the way. I figured since he was white, he may not be as big as my ex-boyfriend. You know the whole stereotype that black men are more endowed. The whole experience was gross and nothing like you see in the movies.

When you are 15, having irregular menses isn't uncommon. I never really thought about why my period wasn't happening for a few months. One morning before school, my mom asked me to pee in a cup. A few minutes later she was telling me I was pregnant. Finding out I was pregnant at the age of 15, after my first time having sex, was like a punishment for all the inappropriate activity I had done over the past few years. Who gets pregnant the first time? Now what were people going to think of me?

I was involved in many activities. Basketball, track, dance team, different social organizations, and of course, church. My mom was angry at me and the situation. She knew that being a teenage mother would be hard for me. It was decided for me that an abortion would be my next step. I didn't want to get rid of my baby. We would go visit an abortion clinic in Lexington, Kentucky. I never said a word, just sat there scared and sad. An ultrasound would determine I was approximately 16 weeks. They would not be able to perform the procedure. Instructing my mom that she could take me to another clinic a little farther away. She would decline. I would be relieved, but my mom would be stressed. The next few months would be filled with tension at my home.

The Mirror of Inner Beauty

My aunt stepped in and took me to my doctor visits, my mom just couldn't let go of the disappointment at first. Keeping life as normal as possible until the school year came to an end proved to be a challenge. Doing things like trying out for the dance team at the end of my freshman year, knowing that I would not be able to go to camp or perform early in the basketball season as my child was due in November. Only a select few of my classmates knew about my secret at the time. As my baby began to grow and kick in my stomach, I started having an unconditional love form for this little person inside of me. What an amazing emotional bond you develop with the little person inside of you. I was going to be a mom and have someone to love me. I vowed to be the best mom for my baby. Picking out names for the baby was exciting. A boy's name was all I focused on. Something in my heart made me feel that I was carrying a boy. Still trying to hide my pregnancy, I began wearing bigger clothes. A white, long sleeve shirt that had panda bears with a red bow around their necks was my favorite top to wear. I didn't really show the whole summer, but I swear on the day before school was to start, I developed a big baby bump. Embarrassed, uncomfortable, and humiliated, I hung my head low the first day of school. Surprisingly to me, my friends didn't shun me or talk badly about me. Instead, they embraced me and my situation and helped me get through a difficult time. The father of the baby would not step forward and claim his responsibility, and I didn't make it known who my son belonged to. There would be whispers and gossip, but I held my head up and tried not to let it bother me. I didn't care because I loved my baby. Everyone was rallying around me with support, and that to me was all my baby needed. He would come into this world on November 28th, 1987, weighing seven pounds, a beautiful, healthy baby, Wesley Shaundale Jones.

Our mother raised us in church, and getting baptized was our decision. My calling to join the church came when I was ten. Disappointment from the church happened after my pregnancy. From the beginning when I found out about the pregnancy, I prayed daily for forgiveness. It didn't occur to me that my church family would make me feel worse than I already did. The pastor at that time felt I needed to stand in front of the church and ask forgiveness for my sins in a room full of sinners. Upset and confused, I left his office. Christians aren't supposed to judge others. What was stating the obvious to a bunch of hypocrites going to do for me? This would begin my not feeling welcomed at my church, and I would distance myself from the one source I believed in.

Being a teenage mom was hard because I had to continue with school and work. It was not my mom's responsibility to get up in the middle of the night for feedings; it was mine. One night I was warming a bottle up on the stove, and Wes went back to sleep before the bottle was warm. I fell asleep as well, so the water boiled off and the bottle began to burn. It set off the smoke detector and woke up everyone in the house. Mom told me I had to be more careful, but she understood I was tired.

My first job was a server at a restaurant; then later, I found a job as a cashier at our local grocery store. My mom helped me a lot, but she also expected me to take care of my child. The responsibility overall was mine. If I wanted to do anything that other high school kids did, like prom or senior trip, I had to pay for these things on my own. Life was confusing, and I wasn't ready for the responsibility that came with this changing situation, but I did the best I could. Blaming myself for bringing my son in the world under these circumstances. This guilt would overshadow and belittle my self-worth.

Hard work and tenacity were my tools for graduating on time. College seemed like a big stretch, but I was going to give it my best. Morehead State University accepted my application and awarded me a small scholarship. Wesley would stay with my mom. The college was close to an hour away from my hometown. The goal was to succeed and make everyone proud.

College brought its own set of rules for fitting in. Still not knowing how to just be me, I fell into the party scene and wild life. Don't get me wrong – I had fun, but some incidents should have never happened. Started out doing great with classes and just hanging with people I knew. Then I started getting invited to parties and hanging out with guys from different fraternities. Insecure about not knowing how to handle myself around guys, I found myself in the same situations I experienced in high school. I started being known around campus as an easy lay, and I was on the hate list of most females. Reality was many of us were being used, but it seemed I was talked about more. All I really wanted was a boyfriend, and I tried hard to find one, but most of the guys were already taken or just looking for fun. But I still had the belief that if I were in a committed relationship, other guys would leave me alone.

One evening I was invited to a private party. This was supposed to be the best party on campus that night. Approaching the apartment, I began to get a weird feeling about knocking on the door. Music was playing inside, so I figured maybe I was a little late and that was why I didn't see anyone else walking to the same place. When the door opened, I recognized most of the guys inside and started to notice I was the only female present. Alone with eight or more guys who were expecting me to service whoever wanted a turn. One by one, they stood there, expecting me to perform some sexual act for them. Screaming out for them to stop, and finally, one guy made them. Distraught, traumatized and broken, I got my clothes and left. You stupid girl, was all I kept telling myself, everything they say about you is true. "You're nothing but a slut, allowing all these guys to use your body. A disgusting piece of trash!" I vowed to never tell anyone about this incident. Tears streamed down my face

The Mirror of Inner Beauty

the whole way back to my dorm room. Hating myself, then memories of being twelve home alone began to resurface. Is there anyone who can help me? When I opened my dorm room, I breathed a heavy sigh. My roommates were gone, so I took a shower and cried without any questions.

After that traumatic incident, I tried to avoid certain people and started keeping to myself. The way I started to view myself and to hear others talk about me was enough to shift me into wanting something better. Pushing the hurt down inside and denying what happened were my survival techniques. After the last semester of that school year was finished, so was I.

Returning home to get my priorities in check. The trauma I had experienced warranted professional help, but I had no idea what resources were available. Being soft was not an option or a solution when you have a child to take care of and need a job. The grocery store rehired me and offered me a full-time position. Dating hadn't been on my radar since returning from college.

Working the courtesy counter gave me a perfect view of the front doors. In walked a guy dressed in work overalls that were unzipped to his waist. A maroon-colored T-shirt and jeans under the work clothes. Sexy as hell to me. Something about him was familiar, then I remembered him from high school. We didn't run in the same crowds, plus he was a few years older than me. Wow, what a total change. He definitely had my nose wide open. He had muscles, a nice stocky build, and was throwing some game my way. We shared a little about each other since graduating, exchanged numbers, and started dating. The more time we spent together, the deeper my feelings became. My first true love, and I had fallen hard for him. The focus was never just about me; my son was included in our relationship. We had been dating about a year when I became pregnant. This was unexpected, being that I was on birth control. Fantasies of him marrying me began to entertain my mind. Becoming our own little family that would be together forever. My thoughts about our life together soon turned into worry. A few months into my pregnancy, he started to become distant. Stated people were saying that the baby wasn't his. How could he say that and believe such bullshit? People get on my nerves, always meddling and wanting to cause drama. My past was the reason for the ugly rumors. It didn't matter how much I pleaded and begged him to believe me; it wasn't enough. My relationship with the love of my life was quickly coming to an end.

I now had to start trying to figure out what I was going to do with two kids. My mother and I had our differences about the outcome of this scenario. She knew I was headed for heartbreak and difficulty. I was still fantasizing about being his wife and living happily ever after. We would be on, then off again. That didn't matter to me, I could fix everything; I just had to be patient.

This turned out to be a long pregnancy. The first due date was my son's birthday, then it changed to December 2nd. This baby enjoyed the warm womb she was growing in and bypassed her due date. She decided to make her debut the day before I was to be induced. When my contractions got close enough to head to the hospital, I called him to meet me, but he was a no- show. My mom stayed with me and gave me support during labor. This labor and delivery proved to be more difficult than my first experience. An epidural was needed to help me endure the pain and relax. After 13 hours of labor, my beautiful chocolate baby girl was born December 7th, 1992, weighing 8 lbs., 12 oz., Alyssa Sherae Davis. When he showed up the next morning to see our daughter, I was furious with him at first. Then I saw how he looked at her, and I knew there was no doubt in his mind she belonged to him.

We would continue trying to date, but he wasn't ready to settle down, and our relationship would end. A father to his daughter would be our only connection. Why was I still holding on to the thought he would come back and things would be better? Depression started to take over my life. I loved him so much, but it wasn't enough. For over a year I was lovesick, waiting for a man who wasn't interested in me. Feelings of not being attractive or deserving began to surface. Devasted and alone with two children, I knew it was time to pull up my big girl panties. I had to start thinking about what was in their best interest. The need to continue my education became a priority. The vocational school in my hometown offered an LPN course. I enrolled and began to think about my future.

Soon after beginning school, I moved out of my mom's house and into a small apartment big enough for me and the kids. It was rough trying to make ends meet, I didn't want to fail at trying to live on my own. Section 8 housing vouchers made my rent manageable, and I qualified for a small amount of food stamps. My caseworker stated I would get more money a month by asking for child support. I had told my daughter's father that I wouldn't seek child support, and my son's dad wasn't in the picture. Decisions needed to be made, and I was running out of options. The child support payments started coming regularly once everything was set up through the court system.

Being a mom, working, and going to school; seems liked I just did this. Sitting up at night crying while my kids slept, trying to understand why I didn't have the life I dreamed about. There were nights of being so tired, and homework wouldn't get done or studying for a test didn't happen. This was going to be a little harder than high school. Honestly, I was just barely passing. My nursing instructor was extra-hard on me. It didn't matter if I had correct answers or spot-on technique, she wanted more. She saw potential and pushed me to not just get by, but to step up to the challenge. Graduation day came, and I was there with my two children, feeling proud of my accomplishment.

After obtaining my LPN license, I secured a job at my local hospital. Finally, I was getting somewhere.

Twenty-four years old with two kids and a career – this was an amazing feeling of redemption. I was able to move into a nicer apartment with my better paying job and get my first brand-new car. It was affordable, a gas saver, and mine. All of this was great, but the longing for love and acceptance still haunted me.

My neighbor had a daughter around the same age as my son, and we became good friends. One night we went out to a local club and her boyfriend introduced me to a friend of his. Good looking black man, muscular, stocky built, and a bald head. Eleven years older than me, but I was attracted to the man. We immediately hit it off and began dating.

My first attempt at having a date night at home didn't go as I had planned. He requested smoked sausage, cabbage, and cornbread. Nervous energy began surfacing because I wanted to make everything perfect. Acting like this was the first time I cooked. Yummy smells started to fill the apartment. The food looked good until I went to sprinkle some pepper on the cabbage and the pepper shaker lid fell off. I was so embarrassed, but he was kind and didn't say anything. Flowers were often given; he was very caring and thoughtful during our courtship. We really had a great thing going. Without me knowing, he had gone and asked my mom for my hand in marriage. He proposed to me on Valentine's day. He sent the kids into the kitchen – one had the ring box and the other had the note. This made me feel complete, and we were going to be a family. We decided on a September wedding until I found out I was pregnant a few weeks later. Determined not to have another child out of wedlock, we moved the wedding up to May. I took control of planning the wedding, getting everything together in such a short time.

The day of the wedding started out crazy. My ex's mother called me that morning and asked me to think hard before marrying this man. Why in the hell would she do that? She would also say that if it rains on your wedding day, that's how many tears you will shed. It had been raining all morning. I was able to compose myself and not let the things she said bother me. We got to the church, and the CD player wouldn't work. This can't be happening; everything was fine last night at the rehearsal. One of the groomsmen had a CD player in his car, and we were able to finish the ceremony without any more problems. Unfortunately, this marriage was not the fairy tale I had fantasized about. Where was the man who said sweet words to me and made me feel special? Dr. Jekyll and Mr. Hyde was who I had married. The verbal, mental, and physical abuse I endured made me terrified to be in his presence. Nothing I did was right; he began yelling at me daily over every little thing. Talking down to me like I wasn't worthy of being in his presence. This was all experienced in the first three months of our marriage. Due to the stress I was going through and trying to work 12-hour nursing shifts, my last child was

The Mirror of Inner Beauty

born at 36 weeks. On October 6th, 1996, weighing 7 lbs., 6 oz. I would have another healthy, beautiful son, Carlton Nicholas Williams.

Getting my tubes tied was what I desired after having my son. To get pregnant by him again would have sent me over the edge. Outraged about my decision, he threatened to sue the doctor if she performed the surgery. My body was his, and I needed his consent, or at least that is what he thought. On the day of my surgery, he didn't take me to the hospital or pick me up, my mother would do this for me. Drowsy and hurting from the procedure, I was still expected to have his dinner ready when he got home.

Depression would start, but I still wouldn't seek help. I just kept on accepting my life would always be this way. Unworthy, damaged, and a doormat for any man to walk on me. When I finally got tired after three years, I filed for divorce. He would fight to keep our marriage, and we had to do counseling, but I had enough, we weren't compatible. I was 27 years old with three kids and enough emotional baggage to be the inspiration for Erykah Badu's song "Bag Lady." Finally, I would break down and ask my doctor for an antidepressant. Dealing with stress and anxiety was becoming difficult. The medication helped me to manage my depression, but to fix my deeper problems, I had no idea where to start. All I needed was for someone to complete me and bring happiness. Used up, three kids who all had different dads made me society's poster child for unworthiness. Lowering my value and such a poor mindset was the pattern I would continue to repeat.

My heart would tell me I was a good person and deserved better. My mind would say I was nothing but a sexual toy for men. No one to speak the truth to me about my behavior, only judgment. The game to use a man for my benefit never worked, I didn't have the skills to turn off my emotions. Instead, I sunk deeper into a self-damaging spiral that would eventually cause me major depression and extreme loneliness.

In 2002, I stepped out on faith and moved from my hometown to provide a better life for my kids. My oldest son stayed with my mom; he was already a sophomore in high school. To uproot him at this point wouldn't have been in his best interest. He was already exhibiting abandonment issues from not having a relationship with his father. Protecting him from my experiences was the main goal. The younger two adjusted well to leaving a small town for the city. I was scared and unsure of the major step I had just taken. But failure would no longer be accepted; survival was my goal.

No one can make you feel inferior without your consent. – Eleanor Roosevelt

Reflecting Self-Judgment

Awakening those hidden pains opens the door to my healing process. Allowing myself permission to validate how I felt about my dad brings peace. A few weeks ago, I went to his grave site and had an emotional release. Regardless of my age, his death made an impact on me, and not acknowledging that for all these years caused me much grief.

Holding on to the guilt and shame from experiencing sexual abuse and my behaviors triggered me to dim my light and hide my inner beauty. We judge others without knowing the complete circumstances around their actions. I was judging myself based on what I thought other people would think of me. Unsure if I deserved any forgiveness, I had lost myself in the sin. Wasn't it my fault, for allowing it to happen? Why did I have to be acting out through promiscuous behavior? I'm still healing from this damage. Insecure and pretending that I was fine when I was disgusted with who I had become. My sons and daughter were my loves, and I was determined to do good by them. They were born because of my decisions, and I carried that burden. Living impatiently, when I needed stability and only found more chaos.

Looking back, I know healing was needed before embarking on any new relationships. I expected each relationship to bring me happiness and fulfillment. Fantasizing about being rescued from my problems and having someone give me the life I desired. Instead, the constant disappointments kept me in the mindset that I needed to settle for whatever attention I was given. By looking to other people for happiness, my identity was lost in the process. Forgiveness was needed for those who wronged me so that I could move on. I didn't know I was a part of that equation. Because I wasn't healed emotionally, I took each damaging wound with me to the next relationship or situation. Projecting on to others what I believed about myself. I allowed whatever abuse I experienced to continue to haunt me and keep me feeling unworthy. Communicating my needs has never been easy. Afraid and timid that my feelings didn't matter to anyone. I didn't speak up because conflict was something to avoid. It made me anxious. Whatever it would take to stay on the good side of others was my focus. Not knowing that doing this was hurting me. The pain was building inside. Producing a volatile explosion that erupted over time. Ignited by a petty remark or incident. That was how I lived for many years. The good thing is that I can now recognize my problems and take the necessary steps to help myself.

Angela Jones-Taul

Your Turn to Reflect
What do you judge about yourself?

The Mirror of Inner Beauty

What a beautiful thing it is, to be able to stand tall and say, "I fell apart and I survived."-unknown

2

THE DARK MASK

Mirror, mirror on the wall, I feel all you do is show my flaws. Never facing the true person I saw, I lived in fear so there I stalled. Will I ever be the fairest of all? Only time will tell with the baggage I haul.

Adjusting to my new life was easy, and the kids seemed happy. It didn't take long for me to realize that working in a nursing home wasn't my forte. Hospitals were phasing LPN's out, and I needed to find something that would have good hours for a single mom. Depression was still a problem for me, and I was trying to deal with things in my own way. Romance novels were my way of curving my appetite to be in a relationship. I could hide myself in the fairy tale and fantasize that I was the woman in the book being swept off her feet. I wasn't brave enough to go and hang out in clubs by myself. Staying single for a while wasn't a bad thing, but I did long to have someone special in my life.

The Mirror of Inner Beauty

Starting my new job as a corrections nurse was exciting and scary. It worked for me because it was different and interesting. Even though I stood out like a sore thumb with my country accent and nice girl persona. I got along with everyone, which has never been a problem for me. Most of the other nurses had street smarts, and they were quick to school me on how to handle myself. The word started getting around that I was single, and I found myself being the center of attention. One day after a med pass, an officer came up to me and asked if I would be interested in seeing a movie with him. I was a little hesitant due to our age difference. He was 11 years younger than me, but I listened to my friends saying, "Girl, get that young meat." I became an official cougar. We started living together about six months after dating. I was making more money than he was at the time, so I took on most of the bills. He was also going back to school for a job promotion. Being a soft-hearted person, I didn't see the need to set any ground rules or expectations for our relationship. One of my many insecure patterns I repeated often.

Things were great until infidelity became an issue on his part. The first time he cheated on me, I let him come back, no problem. The second time we stayed apart for about four months. After a few more years, I grew tired of the game and started demanding some long-term commitment goals. I was in my mid-30s, and I wanted to be married.

After another year of uncertainty, I started going out on my own and had a friend on the side. I figured if he is going to do it, why can't I? He didn't like the tables being turned, so he asked if we could really put forth an effort and be true to each other to make this work. I agreed and stopped my casual fling.

That summer we started planning to buy a house. We began to look at our bills and figure out ways to save money. Our car payments combined were around $700. Mine being the highest at $420. We decided to send my car back. He purchased a cheaper car for me. With his credit being better than mine, the car was put in his name. I would take care of this payment and the insurance. My credit wasn't good, as a result of having filed bankruptcy a few years prior. It also made sense at the time to just let the house be in his name; he was making more money now with his promotion. I instantly fell in love with the home, the previous owner had the backyard landscaped with such beautiful flowers and foliage. It was something off the cover of *Better Homes and Gardens*. My life felt complete; the fantasies I had were starting to show up in real life. Finally getting the things I believed would make me happy.

We were doing great. My kids were in good schools, I had started another job as a staff development coordinator, and I was beginning to take classes to obtain my RN degree; things looked promising. One evening early in December, we went to eat at

The Mirror of Inner Beauty

Outback, just the two of us. It was a brisk evening, he held my hand as we entered the restaurant, I felt special because we hardly ever showed affection in public.

We order some drinks and a blooming onion to begin our dinner. Started having casual conversation, laughing enjoying each other's company. "AJ, I have been thinking about something," he said. "You are so special to me, and I don't ever want to lose you," as he pulls out a ring box. My stomach started to fill with butterflies going crazy inside. "We have been together for a long time, and I think it's time to make this official." He opened the box to reveal the most beautiful, dainty, three-stone princess-cut white gold diamond ring. "Will you marry me?" I was in shock, tears began to form as I squeaked out a yes. He came around the table to give me a kiss. We hadn't noticed the audience of people at first, who were all so happy to congratulate us.

I was so excited! I started taking pictures of my ring and sending them to family. Congratulations started pouring in over text messages. I posted on Facebook, "He didn't go to Jared's, but I said yes anyway." Wow, what an amazing feeling.

After the first of the year, we set a date to be married in August of 2010. I began planning, looking for a wedding gown, deciding on bridesmaids. What an electrifying, stressful time. We paid for the venue, our honeymoon cruise. It was all coming together.

One morning in May, I texted him "good morning" on my way to work; part of our routine. He was on third shift at the time. It wasn't unusual to not get an immediate response. I just figured he was busy wrapping things up. A few hours passed and still no response. I was getting worried since he always texted back. I stepped outside my job to call him, still no answer. This was disturbing. I tried again, no answer.

I went back to my desk and begin to wonder why he wasn't calling or texting. It is now 10 a.m. He returns my call around noon. "Are you ok? I have been trying to reach you all morning, babe." "I'm ok," he said in a low tone. My gut started telling me something isn't right here. I asked, "Are you cheating on me?" Pause. "No, I just have been talking to some fellas and, well, I'm having second thoughts about getting married." I felt like someone had just kicked me in my stomach. I became so nauseous. Tears filled my eyes, but I had to keep it together because I was at work. "I'm going to come home so we can talk." He replied with, "No, I'm not home yet, just stay at work and we can talk later." What the hell just happened? I went numb. My supervisor walked by my office and came in. "Are you okay? You look troubled." I answered, "My wedding is off," and I busted into tears. When I got home and walked into the bedroom, he was packing an overnight bag. "Where are you going?" I asked. "AJ, I don't want to fight. My mind is made up. The wedding is off, and we should think about ending this relationship." "What the fuck is going on with you?" I demanded to know why I was being treated this way. He just looked at me and walked out, just like I was nothing.

This was all unsettling to me, and I needed closure, some answers. I kept calling him until he answered. "What do you want?" I suddenly felt like I was a nuisance. "I just want to talk and work this out. I will do whatever, just don't do this." I begged. This was so pathetic of me. He said goodbye and thought he ended the call, but he didn't. "What's wrong, baby?" a female voice asked. "She still calling you?" I was furious when I heard her voice. I wanted to hunt him down and do serious bodily harm. I texted him, "Don't come home or you will be stabbed." My ego had gotten the best of me, and I was furious with feelings of betrayal. Without having any concrete plans, I took my next two paychecks and secured a place for me and my children. It was not my ideal place, but it was the cheapest and only thing available in the school district. Moving from that home made me feel like I wasn't deserving of nice things. He would never understand the wholeness it brought to me. We had just hosted Thanksgiving for my family, I cooked the whole meal by myself. For me it was a milestone, of stepping into the role my mother had been doing for years. Now I was back to living in an apartment that no one would want to visit.

I started this beautiful sunny day in July of 2010 with no thoughts of having a bad day. A little unusual due to my current situation. I needed to go and run some errands. Out the door and up the steps with a little bounce, humming a tune. "Uh, where's my car?" as I frantically looked around the parking lot. I went back into my apartment and asked my daughter did she know where my car was. She didn't know, "It should be out front," she stated. Now I'm starting to worry someone has stolen my car. Picked up my cell phone to call the police when I got this sensation to contact my ex-fiancé. When I called and asked if he had repossessed the car he calmly stated yes. Envisioning the smirk he had on his face made me angry. "Why in the hell would you take my car?" I yelled into the phone. "How am I supposed to get to work, take the kids places, and get groceries?" His reply was, "I don't know. Figure it out." I went from mad to psycho-crazy in 2.4 seconds. "Ok, since you want to be smart, I'm going to walk to your house and beat your ass." I hung up the phone and started out the door. I was walking so fast my kids were running, trying to catch up to me. "Mom, don't do this, he ain't worth you getting this upset." They were right, but I didn't care. This was it; I was tired of his bullshit. When we broke up, the agreement was that if I kept up with the payments and insurance, I could keep the car. All you have is your word, and he was going back on his promise. Full of angry tears, I stopped and listened to my children and went back to the house. Furious with his actions, I called my mom, sister, and aunt. They all said the same thing: "Let it go, Angie. He's an asshole and stop letting him get to you." Nobody understood I was tired of him controlling the situation. I had nothing anymore, no nice three-bedroom home with two baths, a big yard, a car, a man. All because of him.

The Mirror of Inner Beauty

Sitting on the edge of the bed looking pitiful, angry inside, and crying intermittently. My reflection caught my attention, and I didn't recognize this person. I began to torture myself with the memories of this failed relationship and all my traumas. Where had I gone wrong? Disgusted with myself, I laid down and played out the last seven years in my head.

Now here I lay in a puddle of tears. Seven years of putting up with bullshit, making his life great. Sacrificing my own needs by not hanging around my friends, doing activities I enjoyed, and finishing school. I made it so easy for him to hurt me.

"I can't keep thinking about this," I thought as I sat up and looked in the mirror. "Who are you?" Feeling hopeless, emotionally unstable, and distraught, a sense of doom started to form. My mind began working overtime. I can hear the voice in my head, "You're worthless; a sensitive, spineless, piece of shit." "How do you expect a man would ever want you?" "The only thing you are good for is lying on your back." "That's all you have ever been is a concubine and when they are done with you, they move on." "Take the pills. They are there. You will go to sleep and never wake up. No longer a burden to your kids or family. Face it, you only bring shame. Look how strong you will be to free your family. They won't have to worry about the black sheep anymore because you will be gone. Put them in your hand and swallow, hurry now so it can be over."

My plans were interrupted by a friend as I began to take a handful of Xanax and Ambien. I am forever grateful for her being around. She had stopped over to check on me, knowing that I had been going through a rough time. She took me to the ER for help. I would spend the next week at the Lindner Center of Hope, a mental health treatment center. Let me state that again: a mental health treatment center. I'm not certifiably crazy. Isn't that who usually is sent to these types of places? The negative mindset controlled so much of my life that the idea of taking myself out of this world was my comfort. The constant battle to pretend that I was happy in my life. Always pushing the old wounds down deep, refusing to acknowledge or accept them.

Here I was at this place. Couldn't they understand that I had made a mistake? I no longer wanted to end my life. The intake nurse took me to a small office to complete my admission questions. I felt like a child being sent to alternative school. The nurse took my medical history and have me sign paperwork. The locked unit was written at the top of my papers. She must have noticed my shocked expression and told me not to worry. How could I not worry? I don't belong on a locked, crazy unit. Arriving on my floor, she checked me in at the nurse's station. I was shown the group session room and the commons area where we could watch TV. All I wanted to do was run away and go home. Everything was nice and up to date with style, but I didn't want to be there. This was a nightmare that needed to end. Tears began to fill my eyes. What kind of mess had I created now?

The Mirror of Inner Beauty

Down the hall to the left was a lonely room that felt like a jail cell. A twin-size bed, no TV, and a small window to look out of. Taking a shower could only happen when I requested the water to be turned on in my room. All my personal hygiene stuff was kept at the nurse's station. No wigs or hair products with me, and no one could bring me anything. I looked like a hot mess.

As part of the rules, we were required to eat as a group on the unit. You had to earn privileges to eat by yourself in the cafeteria. The next morning after breakfast, I was introduced to everyone on my floor during the first group session. In my mind, I was thinking this whole time these women have serious issues, mine are minor. What I didn't understand was we all shared relatable experiences. It didn't matter if you were anorexic, a cutter, or suffering from depression. We still needed to admit our flaws.

My therapist from the center was a caring, empathetic soul who listened to me describe my Lifetime Movie events. In one of our sessions, she stated I was grieving the loss of the relationship, but she felt I was holding on to something else. I thought about what she said, I just didn't know how to figure out what it meant.

When my family came to visit me, I felt ashamed. Seeing the worry and concern on their faces made me want to cry. They offered support and help for when I got out. Told me to forget all the bullshit and move on. What they didn't understand was it wasn't that simple for me. I've always felt like the black sheep of the family. The oddball, the one who always had something going on. Seeing them look at me as if I were a lost cause touched my soul and I knew I would have to find a way to get better.

I followed the protocol of taking my medication and participating in my therapy sessions in order to be released. This incident stayed in my head for a long time. The feelings of being a weak individual would begin to resurface. Using my brave mask to help hide my true feelings of being scared, praying that everyone would just forget what I had done. Life was rough for a while. I still needed the medication for anxiety and sleep. Carefully making sure I used them for their intended purpose or not taking them at all. Since the broken engagement, I moved three times and lived in areas that were not in my comfort zone. Survival started to become harder for me, and I was barely making ends meet. My ex-husband suggested our son live with him until I could get myself together. That was hard to let him go, yet it did make sense. My daughter was 17 and a senior in high school, independent and resilient. My focus was to get her to college and push her to be better than me.

I had no money to get a vehicle at that time, but lucky for me, my job as a school nurse was about two and a half miles from my apartment. Walking to work brought a daily crying spell. Mainly because I was hurt, but other times were due to going past the street where I had lived with my ex. My mind

The Mirror of Inner Beauty

would begin to play out scenarios of how happy they must be together in that nice house. It was unfair, and I wanted him to suffer.

I was embarrassed to ask for help at first, but when it started to get cold, the walks became difficult. I reached out to a few people at my job and was able to get a ride with a coworker. Asking for help was hard; I wanted to be strong and recover on my own. Believing that showing vulnerability would make me appear weak, I refused to reach out to my support system. Family and friends would always offer help – I just needed to accept the invitations. When I finally did, doors opened, and my struggles didn't keep me weighed dow

Angela Jones-Taul

Stepping onto a brand-new path is difficult, but not more difficult than remaining in a situation which is not nurturing to the whole woman.
-Maya Angelou

The Mirror of Inner Beauty

Reflecting Self-Hatred
Remembering that painful day brings tears, not because I felt so distraught, but because I can still feel my family and close friends' deep concern for me. In my mind, I have always been a disappointment. No one has ever said that to me; It's my own thoughts and feelings about myself. I set the expectation and standards so high that when I didn't reach them, it devastated me. Striving to cover up the imperfections I believed about myself, I often combined a little of my true self with different versions of who everyone else wanted. When I first really looked in the mirror that day, I hated the reflection. All I could imagine was every single disappointment I had in my life. Hating myself for not being strong enough to walk away from relationships that weren't healthy. Ignoring reality, hoping that my issues would go away. My pain was buried deep inside and behind a mask. When I felt my true self trying to emerge, I sabotaged myself because I was afraid to be me. The mirror held my truth that I desperately wanted to hide. When would I get out of this pattern? I still was not seeing the real issue. How do I live for me?

These were questions that I had no idea how to find answers to. Praying daily that I hadn't messed my life up by being this person I truly didn't know. I didn't want to be a victim and have everyone feeling sorry for me. I wanted freedom and purpose. To be seen and heard. Questioning all my life's decisions and beating myself up – this was no longer acceptable to me. I not only needed to find a solution, I had to be the solution.

Life is a mirror and will reflect back to the thinker what he thinks into it. – Ernest Holmes

Angela Jones-Taul

Your Turn to Reflect
How does your inner critic affect you?

3
PEELING AWAY THE MASK

Mirror, mirror on the wall, how do I stop the tears that fall? My mind is a battlefield and I'm afraid I won't win. A wounded goddess is not how this shall end.

A fresh start is what I needed after the suicide attempt and a year of feeling lost. I wasn't sure what needed to be done, but I knew feeling sorry for myself and online dating weren't the answer. My actions were making me become desperate for a man. Losing respect for myself, I was going out every chance I could with whoever seemed liked a good prospect, only to be disappointed by lies and rejection if I didn't have sex on the first date. Feeling so alone again, my kids weren't there to keep me focused or motivated. Slowly falling back into repetitive patterns of depending on others to need me, to keep me grounded and sane. Consumed with fixing other people's lives had me forgetting what I enjoyed doing for fun. Friends became distant due to me shutting them out. Asking for help was such a scary concept for me. The embarrassment of my actions kept me worried about what everyone was saying about me.

One of the few people I call a good friend had been after me for months to attend church with her. I made excuses as to why I couldn't. Condemnation and unworthy feelings filled my heart and mind. Made me think that I was no longer able to attend church after my sinful ways. On the evening of their super Sunday, I needed to drop something off to her. She told me to just come by the church and drop it off. I thought I would just drive up, she would come out, and that would be it. Well no, she told me to park and bring it in. This was a casual set up, and the women were sitting in a room mingling. When I got to the area, they were just getting ready to have a small group discussion and, of course, I couldn't be rude and just leave. I'm not sure what the topic of discussion was, but I found myself weeping and being touch deeply in my soul. I know I was filled with the Holy Spirit that evening. These women had no idea what I had endured over the past few months, but they spoke words of encouragement and strength to me. After that, I began attending church regularly, and my negative thoughts stopped consuming me. How had I lose sight of the one constant in my life? My faith has always been a source of healing, but because I was aligning myself with people who didn't have as deep of a belief, I was led astray easily.

The Mirror of Inner Beauty

Working for the school system was nice, but the pay wasn't what I was used to making. Getting a part-time job would help, but it still wasn't even close to getting me where I had been a year ago. Bills started to pile up, and I sometimes would have to choose between keeping the lights on or eating. Many times I wondered how someone gets to the point where they are homeless, and here I was, so close to that point. Easily I could've stayed with my sister or gone home to stay with mom, but I was tired of having others help me. Pride kept me from asking for help when my electricity was shut off for a week. After I got home from work, I would sit in my apartment alone and eat a peanut butter sandwich until the daylight disappeared. Going from room to room and surveying my belongings. I had a secondhand love seat, a table and two chairs in the kitchen, and an air mattress in my room. No one there to talk with or comfort me and tell me everything would be fine. Some days I would get my Bible out to read while I could with the sunlight. I didn't know what was going to happen, but I had faith everything would work out.

One day at work on my lunch break, I called my aunt crying and telling her I could feel the dark cloud of doom starting to show up again. She suggested that maybe I should move, get away from the constant reminders of what I had been through. Praying that my decision to move would be the best thing to do, I sent out resumes for jobs in places that would get me away from Cincinnati. One month later, I would receive a call from a clinic in Lexington, KY and we set up an interview. Going into the interview, I felt confident I would get the job, but there was a process, so I would be invited back for a second interview.

Cable or Internet didn't fit with my current financial situation, so I would go to the local library to use the computer and check the online dating site. Just as I was getting ready to delete my profile, I began conversing with a guy who lived in Lexington, KY. We had a lot in common. He had been in a bad relationship a year ago and was looking for something different. On our first phone call, we talked for hours. Laughing often as we began sharing stories and similar interests. I started out lying at the bottom of my bed, then sitting on the floor, then back on the bed with my feet against the wall. I was giddy and felt like a teenager in high school. Could it be possible I found my soulmate?

On 11/11/2011, I packed my car with only my clothes and a few personal belongings and headed to Lexington, KY to live. When I was offered the job, I took it as a sign that I was headed in the right direction. No more nights of beating myself up about the past. I was determined to do better. My daughter was in college, and this move would put me closer to my youngest son. I stayed with family until I got settled in my new job and found my own place. Things were great. For once, I felt like I the bad luck cloud was finally leaving me.

I had only been in my own place a couple of months when my daughter who was five months pregnant pleaded with me to let her come live with me. I allowed her to come stay because I knew how hard being young and pregnant can be, and you needed your mom. My boyfriend and I were still doing good, not rushing things; he still lived with his mom and I was fine with him trying to establish himself. We did traditional dating stuff: going to the movies, bowling, and attending local college sports games. We could make an evening sitting at home watching TV, the best time ever. Do I dare start daydreaming of spending my life with this man?

Nursing was taking a toll on me, and I was getting burned out. Working in the clinic was great; I just still hadn't learned about setting boundaries. Taking on more responsibilities than I needed. Still trying to prove my worthiness. My expectations for how I felt the workplace should be would eventually push me to a stressful breaking point. An overnight stay in the hospital for an irregular heart rhythm got me thinking about getting out of the nursing field. My passion is to help people, and before I had moved, my interest in massage school began to surface. Continuing with that plan, I started school in the part-time program for massage therapy. Excitement and a newfound energy began to stir inside. I was thrilled about being in the course, and I formed a family with my fellow classmates. Most of the courses were a reminder for me from nursing, but learning about energy work and holistic wellness is what I loved the most. Getting through massage school was challenging because I had to work full-time, help my daughter, and nurture a relationship. I found myself wanting to give up and quit. Why couldn't I just stick with nursing and be happy? I found strength in knowing that massage was a calling for me. I just kept telling myself to graduate, and then I could start my own massage therapy practice.

My relationship was starting to fizzle out. We lost that initial connection, or at least I was feeling like we didn't click anymore. Being second to a video game was not my speed. Comparing my past men problems to what was going on now made everything confusing. My whole identity revolved around sex because that's how I got attention. He was neither bothered nor impressed about it, and that was new for me. This made me wonder if he truly liked me, maybe I wasn't sexy after all. I decided we needed to break up. Wow, I couldn't believe I was wanting to end a relationship; something was changing in me. I was starting to want more for myself.

We had been apart for about two months when he called me over to see him at his mom's house. "Babe, can I still call you that?" he asked. We shared an awkward giggle. "You are the best thing to come into my life, I have lost my best friend, and I want her back." He gets down on one knee and pulls out a ring box. "Will you marry me?" As I looked down at this beautiful solitaire diamond ring, my heart jumped, and tears began to fall. "Yes, I will marry you." He stood up, wiped my tears, and kissed me. Time to let everyone know again that I was engaged.

Finally moving forward. I was engaged, had a great job, and was embarking on a new career, but something was missing. A nagging feeling in my gut started. Making me feel like I was about to make a huge mistake in my relationship. We had a lot in common, but ideally, we were further from being right for each other than I wanted to realize. He was a great man, but I wasn't happy. The initial connection and synchronicity were gone. I started seeing his true nature – nothing horrible like my past; I just wanted something more. Getting married because I believed it would complete me wasn't the answer. Putting an end to the engagement and relationship felt like I had made the best decision for myself and him.

My life shifted again and became stressful. My daughter became pregnant again soon after having the first baby. All the hard work I had done to get back on track just unraveled. All I wanted was some stability. The stress was that I couldn't handle taking care of everyone. Now my daughter's boyfriend was living with us, and another baby was on the way. I would have to show some tough love after grandbaby number two arrived. Telling my daughter they would need to find their own place. My advice to her was that it would probably be best for her to move back to our hometown because the cost of living was cheaper.

She didn't like that at first, but I had to start saying no or I was going to lose my sanity. My plan to transition into massage full time didn't go very smoothly. My massage clientele wasn't building fast like I thought it would, and the nursing position pay wasn't enough to pick up the slack. Money was tight, and I found myself struggling to pay bills. I moved back in with family again to get myself on track. If you are following me, then you know what came next – correct, another relationship about a year later. I started seeing a guy from another dating site; he lived in Cincinnati. I know you are probably thinking when is she going to learn?

He wasn't much of a phone-talking person, so we did a lot of text messaging back and forth. Our first date, he came to Lexington to see me. We met at Cheddar's restaurant to eat. He was a handsome gentleman, tall and nicely built, and he was white. Game changer – thought I would switch my preference since I wasn't having luck with the black males. After dinner, we drove around Lexington sightseeing. It was still early and decided to go see the movie *Three Days to Kill*. What an amazing evening, and to end it perfectly, all he did was kiss me on the forehead. No expectation for sex or even a discussion.

We started to see each other on weekends if our schedules permitted, and some during the week. The hour and half drive was an issue, but when you are smitten you don't mind. I began to research jobs again in Cincinnati, thinking being closer to him would be better, and I needed a better paying job. My dreams about opening my own massage business was put on the back burner.

One of the positions I applied for showed interest rather quickly. My first interview went well, and a second interview that would take place a few weeks later did too. The job offer letter came a few days after my last interview. Praying my decision to accept was the right one, I began to make plans to move again. Excited to start this new job and strengthen my relationship.

In July of 2014, I moved back to the northern Kentucky/Greater Cincinnati area and stayed with my sister until I got settled in my own place. Once again, looking for the stability, love, and acceptance I so strongly desired. Feeling this time things would be different, not realizing how true this statement would be. The job was different for me; I wasn't hands-on like my past nursing positions. This was more case management, desk work, and patient advocate.

One gorgeous sunny August day, on my way home from work, I received a voice mail. I was sitting in standstill traffic on I-75 S, so I thought this would be a good time to listen. It was a Dear Angela letter. He left me a voice mail stating he was sorry, but his estranged wife and he were going to reconcile. "What the hell did he just say?" I said out loud, like someone was in the car with me. Restarting the message again to make sure I heard him correctly. They had spent the weekend together and rekindle the old flame. On his profile he listed he wasn't married, and the times I stayed with him there were no indications that he was. I found myself thinking, you fucking idiot, girl when are you going to catch a clue? My first instinct was to try and call him, but I knew he would never answer. Needing to vent, I called my aunt and cried to her over the phone. She told me to get it together – I had to drive home, no need to get upset, it would all work out, and to call her later. How was I supposed to get it together? He lied to me. This was unacceptable. I needed answers; I deserved that, right?

As soon as I got home, I did leave him a voice mail back stating that this was a cowardly and shitty way to end things, but I understood and wished him and his wife the best. Morally I knew it was wrong to want a man who was married, but here I was, emotionally attached. This left me feeling bitter and betrayed; all he had to do was be honest. Now what was I going to do? This pattern of living for others was starting to wear me down. Here I was again, adjusting my life to fit into someone else's. When would I start to see the big picture?

One Sunday my sister invited me to the church she goes to, and the message touched my soul. I just felt an urge to take a stand and unload my burden. I knew then it was time to root myself back into church.

Joining a women's small group that was based on the book by Joyce Meyer, *Battlefield of the Mind,* was my first step. Getting involved in this group opened up my mind to seeing that I was in a very toxic

The Mirror of Inner Beauty

relationship with myself. It made me start to question my actions and speak about my life situations. For over 20-plus years, I have been struggling with the emotional baggage from my abuse and teenage pregnancy. Still holding on to the guilt and unforgiveness for myself. I had managed to make my own mess that included low self-esteem, anxiety, depression, and unhappiness. None of these actions made my life easier. It was nice for once to be surrounded by supporting, empowering women who were going through similar situations. Being able to be vulnerable without judgment.

Reading this book and working with the group helped stir up my soul. The emotional stir I was feeling was uncomfortable, but I was beginning to see that I was more than what I had allowed myself to be. The limits I placed on myself in so many ways. Trapped in my thoughts, wanting to end the people-pleasing aspect of my personality. More personal work than reading a few books was needed to retrain my mindset.

The loneliness feeling began to resurface again, and I started doing online dating once more. Why? Because I had no idea that the love I so desired needed to come from me. Nothing had changed; most of the men still only wanted the easy hookup, and the others were emotionally unavailable. One evening while sitting on my couch, I began crying, begging for a change, I didn't want to be this person anymore. Here I was sitting alone, feeling unloved, and hurting. Reminding myself of the past trauma that still plagued my thoughts. Finally telling myself I was abused, plain and simple. That I needed to understand that I wasn't a 12-year-old anymore feeling trapped and unprepared. Praying and hoping that a light would shine on my path. Forcing myself to look in the mirror at this fragile person. Knowing that my purpose in this world was not about being a pushover or a doormat. Telling myself to hang in there, better days were coming. I could feel it in my soul.

A tragic accident happened to a friend of my ex's. I reached out to him through a text message just to show support and sympathy. He wanted to thank me for being so caring. I told him it wasn't necessary, but he insisted. We met for something to eat, and he began to tell me that he had made a mistake with trying to work things out with his wife. I told him that it wasn't a mistake, and he would've been more upset with himself if he hadn't. He agreed and complimented me on being a good listener and person. Even though he had lied to me, my feelings for him were still strong. It would only take a few weeks before he began to contact me daily.

That initial spark we had was still there, and I gave in to him, wanting to try again. He was still married and wasn't sure when they would start divorce proceedings. Some people would not get hung up on this technicality, but it did make me uncomfortable and became a source of strife for us. What I noticed was that I no longer wanted to tolerate his manipulative ways.

The Mirror of Inner Beauty

The next segment of small groups started up at church and introduced me to another group of special women who were placed on my path to continue helping me build my self-image. We studied the women of the Bible and how we relate. I formed a close bond with these women. My birthday was coming up soon, and they decided for my gift to pay my way to the Women's Conference that was coming up at the church. What an amazing, uplifting, spiritual experience and wonderful time we had. They help me to see the damaging effects of the relationship I was involved in at the time. My self-worth was important; if trying to better myself and heal was a threat to him, then I didn't need him. He wanted me to stay wounded; that way his faults would be minimized. He knew I had a poor view of myself, and I allowed him to use it against me. This relationship introduced me to learning about narcissists and their manipulative ways.

I told myself over 100 times that I would break this cycle. No longer would I put my wants and needs on hold. Change was the answer, but hard to achieve. Honestly, I wasn't even sure where to begin.

Angela Jones-Taul

***You teach people how to treat you by what you allow, what you stop, and what you reinforce.
– Tony Gaskins***

The Mirror of Inner Beauty

Reflecting Self-Respect

During this time of transition, I would begin to understand I was starting to grow. The failed engagements and relationships were learning tools. I wouldn't see it at first, but reflecting helped put it all in perspective. I was finally seeing that I did have a choice. I needed to feel comfortable with myself. Trying to cover up old wounds that were only visible to me, this allowed the abuse to control my outlook of myself. I had to hear myself say that I was abused, and I was 12. That I am responsible for my actions later in life and accept that I should have made better choices. I wished time and time again to be different. This would be the starting point of recognizing that I didn't have to give my precious goods away for meaningless affection from men. The concept of respecting myself to get respect was hard. I didn't understand that I was still suffering from my early trauma. I gave freely and was used. I loved deeply and was abused. I trusted but was naïve. I listened and lost my voice.

I hadn't developed total confidence in myself. I would change my values to suit someone else. My fears of not being love took power over my life, and not facing them kept me stuck in unhealthy, repetitive relationships. I needed to accept that the people who were manipulating and using me would retaliate because of my changes. I needed to be comfortable with going against the norm. I am different, and that is okay. Who I wanted to be was wrapped up so tightly in other people, I thought I had no way to escape. Afraid that people would judge me for wanting more.

Respecting myself so others would give me respect. Seeing different perspectives and ultimately taking responsibility.

The Mirror of Inner Beauty

You've been criticizing yourself for years and it hasn't worked. Try approving of yourself and see what happens. – Louise Hay

Angela Jones-Taul

Your Turn to Reflect
Do you accept less than what you deserve?

4
THIS IS ME

Mirror, mirror on the wall, if you only knew how hard this mask is to haul. I draw the line, it must end. My inner beauty wants to win.

In my current state of being, I wasn't happy. After ending my relationship again, I found myself being more depressed and anxious, and panic attacks were the norm. A daily overwhelming feeling became the routine at my job. The coworker who shared my workload retired, and it would be six months before they found a replacement. My patience was nonexistent, and people were getting on my nerves. I couldn't understand why everyone else wasn't putting in the same amount of extra work that I was. I would agree to do a certain task knowing that I really didn't have the time. Drawing blood, giving injections, and rooming patients was an enjoyment for me but not part of my specific job routine. It wasn't my responsibility to always pick up the slack, but I did it anyway. Then I would get upset at everyone else because I put my expectations on them. I was the overachiever looking for acceptance and validation. When I didn't receive it, I felt like I was being done wrong. Why couldn't they see my struggle? All I wanted was to be noticed and appreciated.

Unfortunately, this was nothing new for me. This was the typical scenario for many years. Get excited about starting something new, telling myself I was going to stick with my decisions. Only to discover I was dissatisfied and not living how I wanted because I was comparing myself to others. Taking medication was not something I enjoyed doing, but when tears started falling daily, getting back on them was needed. When this feeling would resurface, the anxiety would get out of control and if I didn't get a handle on it, I could easily slip back into a severe depression. Going down that road again was not an option.

My family doctor suggested I see a therapist that specialized in women issues. She taught me about setting boundaries with family, friends, and work. Learning to say no and being okay with that decision. Not allowing others to guilt me into doing a task that I had no desire doing. I still hadn't found the confidence to use my voice unless I was extremely upset. Constantly explaining myself to others, telling my side of how I was done wrong in certain situations. In other words, I was complaining. How did I get to be like the very people I was complaining about? Easy; I was projecting. I thought I was just expressing my

The Mirror of Inner Beauty

feelings, but it became the same story all day long to four different people either at work or at home.

For years I watched my peers and friends go back to school and get their RN degrees. Their lives seemed to be awesome, and I based my career on theirs. I attempted to go back to school for nursing, only to fail because it wasn't my true calling. Massage was my desire, but because success wasn't instant, I gave up. Building up my clientele would require effort on my part, not just sitting and waiting. A transition was happening, but I didn't realize just yet what that meant.

The nursing position that I was in would help me to see more about myself. I needed the maturity of the position to open my eyes to accepting my limits. I had no idea that I was standing in the way of my own progress by staying in a victim role. Although the therapist was helping, I still felt as if I needed to dig deeper into myself. I felt stuck in my personal and work relationships. Around my coworkers, I joked to them that I needed a life coach to help me figure out my dysfunctional self. We would laugh, but inside I knew this to be a true statement.

Facebook would be the door to me finding my coach. Through one of my massage classmates, I sent a friend request to a respected massage therapist who was also a life coach. She was offering some free webinars about a group coaching session via the web. Learn about what causes you to be stuck, find purpose in your life, gain clarity were the words that caught my interest. This was right up my alley, the universe was placing this opportunity in front of me, and I accepted.

Taking this step to help myself would put me on the path to my spiritual journey. What she provided me were tools to help unlock the blocks I had placed on myself from living in fear. Just like the tiny pair of glasses that gave me such clarity, I began to really see things more clearly. I became part of a mastermind group with people who were going through similar setbacks. These women came from all different backgrounds and experiences and offered me so much more than a licensed therapist. It has been absolutely the best investment.

Learning from others' insights opened my mind and heart. My hunger for the knowledge to help unlock the blocks I was experiencing kept growing. During a group webinar, my coach mentioned about how a person can get caught up in the victim mentality. This statement hit a nerve, and on our next one-on-one session, I asked her to explain. Realizing I was this person was a shock to me. I never imagined that I wasn't living in 100 percent gratitude. A constant complainer instead of being grateful when good things happened, my focus was always on the bad. I had always thought I had a right to complain and used it as a crutch. It was also in this session that I named my sabotaging voice. I call her Esther. My inner child who helped me when I was younger. She kept me in the "comfort zone" that I had become accustomed to so that I could survive. We were afraid to move forward because we didn't know how to take the first steps. I needed to embrace Esther and talk to her. This sounds crazy and bizarre, but it helped me. All the issues and patterns that kept showing up over and over were about me facing my fears. Most were in personal relationships, other times, my jobs. It was a constant battle I wanted to change, but fear kept me slipping back. The suggestion for me to read *Codependent No More*, by Melody Beattie had come up several times. I had no idea I was suffering from being codependent. Once I read the book, the light bulb and aha moments started to make sense. Reading the book gave me a deeper understanding of how being codependent controlled every aspect of my life. My mood, life, decisions all revolved around what would make other people happy. My dreams, social surroundings, activities I enjoyed were put to the side by staying in this needy mindset. Stability was what I wanted, but being impatient kept me in chaos.

Several months went by without me dating anyone. One weekend I was hanging out with a close friend, and we went to attend the yearly "court day event," a huge outdoor flea market. I ran into an old friend who has always had a crush on me. He asked if I was dating anyone or hung up on someone. I answered no, and for once it felt great to be free of lingering emotional baggage. He whispered in my ear that I would be his. "Let's keep it real." I found that statement very cocky and whispered back, "We shall see." We began dating; he would make the drive to

Cincinnati from Richmond, KY, to visit me on weekends. He was attentive and caring, I became smitten quickly. One evening before he went to work, we were talking on the phone and he asked me when I wanted to become his wife. I stated, "When are you going to ask me?" He wasn't the most romantic guy, but he got his point across.

Early in December, we were going to the mall to do some Christmas shopping. Once inside the mall, he directed me to Kay Jewelers. Clueless to what was going on. He stopped in front of the engagement rings and asked me to pick out my ring. Let me explain something – I have never been a flashy type of girl, so I had already scoped out a ring at Walmart that I wanted very badly. He told me he would never buy a woman he loves a ring from there.

The clerk came over to assist us. I was so nervous; I wanted a pretty ring but didn't want him to spend too much. She asked, "What type of style do you like?" Being indecisive, I answered, "I'm not sure, I like the princess cuts and baguettes in the rings." She pulls out this beautiful three-carat princess-cut white gold ring with baguettes down the side to show me. I gasped, "This is beautiful; how much?" When she said, "$6,000," I politely gave it back. She said, "Hold on, I have it in a smaller carat," and this was more in the price range I felt comfortable with him paying. You know what time it was: bragging time. Family and social media, here I come. We were married on March 25, 2017. We had a very small ceremony with

The Mirror of Inner Beauty

just our immediate family and a nice reception with family and friends. We had a great time. I felt like everything had really lined up for me this time.

The desire to open my own massage business was still nagging me. School had only provided me a bare minimum on how to run a business. I had no extra money saved up, but in my gut, it felt like the time was now for me to pursue my desire. Researching other therapists and the Internet, I started the process to begin my dream. The decision to open my business in my hometown of Maysville, KY was an easy one. By already working on Saturdays at a salon located there, I had already begun building a small clientele.

September of 2017, I opened Pure Touch Massage Center. My availability was two days a week at first because I was still working as a nurse. In January of 2018, I went full time with massage and for once put nursing to the side. My husband was not happy about moving, but I couldn't handle driving over an hour back and forth. If I had it all to do over again, I may have done some things differently, but stepping out on faith was all the reassurance I needed. There were plenty of days where it seemed like I had made the biggest mistake of my life. From my previous attempt, I knew that success was not an overnight thing, and I had to trust the process. Old patterns and Esther would start to send me into a downward spiral. The constant overthinking and worrying made me anxious. Second-guessing every forward step I had taken, but I continued pressing on and reiterating to myself

I can do this. A tremendous amount of growth in such a short time made me feel like I was on a crazy merry-go-round.

My marriage went through a series of growing pains, and I wasn't sure that we had a solid enough foundation to last. I was changing, finally having the courage to join my dark side with the light. All this self-discovery was new to me, and I didn't quite know how to manage it. My husband wanted my love and attention. I was still trying to love myself. We would make mistakes and be hurtful. I would focus on his faults and negative ways. I was allowing others to get in my head and tell me I needed to leave him. I was ready and had a plan in motion to end my short marriage.

Then I thought about how I truly felt; we weren't communicating well, I was changing but for the better. I was being one-sided, and unfair. He only had some information about my past, but he had no idea how truly lost I was and how much I needed to find myself.

Once we eliminated outside influences and focused on what our marriage needed to be founded on, things got better. I just needed to believe what others saw in me, a beautiful woman.

The Mirror of Inner Beauty

Comparison is the thief of Joy.
— Theodore Roosevelt

Reflection Self-Acceptance

The beauty of acknowledging Esther helped me to identify and begin to accept who I am. I no longer avoided understanding my hurts and hang-ups. Learning about being codependent and accepting the truth of the meaning spoke volumes. Being codependent means you support or enable another individual's manipulative, controlling behaviors. You need their approval or validation. You compromise values, choices, and personal well-being. In other words, this is who Angela Dawn Jones-Taul was. The amount of growth I experienced from late 2016 to the present has been so uplifting. Bad days come and go. They no longer stay around for weeks and months. Esther and I have conversations that would make most people think I needed medication.

Doesn't matter what others think, I'm living my life for me now. This doesn't make me selfish or arrogant. It makes me a stronger and more self-reliant woman. Accepting who I am and identifying my beauty has released me from the old perceptions of myself. Having the realization that a change needed to happen within myself helped me to grow. I was still so worried about not having every aspect of my life in perfect harmony. I wanted everything – a husband, house, car, and a career. I was willing to accept it at any cost, even my own sanity.

There are still many aspects of my life that I'm learning to accept, and I can honestly say that I'm enjoying the discovery. It has given me peace and

The Mirror of Inner Beauty

motivation to continue my journey. My coach would often ask me what my "why" was for wanting this change and writing this book. It took me awhile to really pull the answer from my heart. I just wanted to be me and feel comfortable with honoring myself. By shutting off my true desires to accommodate others, I lost myself, and now I'm awakening.

Angela Jones-Taul

Your Turn to Reflect
Do you compare yourself to others?

5
I'M ALIVE

Mirror, mirror on the wall, you reflected what I perceived.
My mind was unhealthy, and I see that now.
Let's be friends and live at ease.

Living with stress, depression, and anxiety takes a toll on your body. I found myself experiencing illnesses, fatigue, weight gain, and not having much energy to do anything. From early in 1996 after the birth of my youngest son until 2018, I was on some form of antidepressant. Taking these meds made me feel like I was weak for not being able to deal with life. Stopping them made me think I could handle what life was showing me. The fall and winter months would prove to be the hardest months to go without medication. I was diagnosed with having seasonal affective disorder.

I would go see a therapist when I felt like I was slipping into an uncontrollable mind frame, but I didn't stick with any regimen. I still was allowing society's conditioning that being vulnerable was a sign of weakness to control me.

I didn't get serious about getting my act together until mid-2015. That's when I had started seeing the therapist who talked to me about setting boundaries. She also reminded me about using guided imagery meditation. When I learned about that in massage school, it had been so relaxing and centering. A health coach had been offered through my employer to help me with my diabetes, hypertension, and nutritional counseling. I started to see a difference in my overall well-being once I put my health first. Losing weight is still a struggle, and I'm actively seeking ways to shed the pounds.

In January of 2018, I decided to approach my health and wellness in a different way. I wanted to cleanse my mind and body from medications. I stopped taking my antidepressants, sleeping medicine, blood pressure meds, and diabetic meds. I don't recommend anyone do this without consulting their doctor first.

I started meditating and stepping back to reflect before responding. I began to think about myself and what I wanted. I, for once, was not apologizing for being who I am. I'm not saying this is an easy task; it takes commitment and desire to change.

About six months after stopping my meds, I went to the doctor for a checkup. I was doing great, but my blood pressure was creeping back up again, so I decided to go back on my med. Everything else was fine – blood sugars were lowered, no panic attacks. Self-care was working, and I intended to keep it going.

It wasn't just about taking a proactive step toward my health but also incorporating a new outlook for my life. Keeping a journal, decluttering my life, letting go of negative people, and most importantly, living my best life. Decreasing my time on social media helped me to not feel so pressured to compare myself. Whenever I stay on Facebook too long, I find myself in my own personal pity party. It takes some effort at times to stop scrolling through other people's posts. My goal is to focus on my groups and posting inspirational quotes. A positive mindset changed how I wanted my reflection in the mirror to be. Living with an attitude of gratitude helps keep the worry and stress at bay. I can complain about anything and everything, but what an amazing, uplifting tool gratitude has become for me.

I began reading more self-help books on shadow work and finding your inner goddess. My interest in improving my mindset was becoming a priority. Another important tool that I had overlooked was the power of forgiveness. Not so much for the person who had wronged me, but to forgive myself. Because of my faith, I knew that it was a necessary step to forgive someone so that I could move on and be set free. The concept of letting myself off the hook was an entirely different hurdle. When I began my coaching sessions, my coach reminded me that I hadn't let go, and that was weighing me down. That's when I wrote my love letter to myself. I cried like a baby; the tears represented healing and growth.

My first step was to search for groups locally that I could seek help from. Immediately after we moved to Maysville, I found myself a church home. I was determined to stay grounded in my faith. Crosspoint Community Church welcomed me and offered me inspiration. I serve regularly as a greeter and recently became part of the Celebrate Recovery group. Most people think this is just for those who have alcohol or drug problems, but it's for anyone with a habit, hurt, and hang-up. I truly feel blessed to have found this group and privileged they have asked me to be a group leader. Who would have thought that someone with low self-esteem and low self-worth would be an asset to a program for helping others with similar issues?

The Mirror of Inner Beauty

***An empty lantern provides no light. Self-care is
the fuel that allows your light to shine brightly.
– Unknown***

Reflecting Self-Care

It's hard to remember how many times I told myself I was going to try and do better for myself. In my coaching sessions, I would soon learn that speaking words like "try" kept me from committing to change. I would allow fear (false evidence appearing real) to overshadow me. I knew how to help everyone else, but when it came time for me, I drew a blank. What stands out to me the most about self-care is I have always been an advocate for promoting health and wellness. Here I was, unhealthy in all areas of my life. For some reason, doing things for myself seemed like such a selfish act, but it was a much-needed step. Getting caught up in the routines of life depleted my energy levels, leaving me susceptible to illnesses and mental anguish.

Actively recognizing the need to focus on my needs helped to support my dreams and desires. It wasn't an easy thing to implement, but once I started making small changes, I noticed how much happier and healthier I was. It all boils down to having an ultimate love for yourself.

I had been in the caregiver role for so long, the thought of me being selfish about my needs was not an easy task. Just simple things like taking a bubble bath, getting my hair done on a regular basis. It was difficult for me to understand that it was okay to indulge in these acts. I often forget and get caught up in the hustle and bustle of life, but it doesn't take long

The Mirror of Inner Beauty

for me to realize that I have neglected some of my basic needs. This usually results in healthcare issues, weight gain, and stress.

Angela Jones-Taul

Healing isn't about changing who you are; it's about changing your relationship to who you are. A fundamental part of that is honoring how you feel. – Suzanne Hey

The Mirror of Inner Beauty

Self-Care Challenge
Commit to a self-care plan

- Take ten deep breaths in and out in the morning and before bed.
- Write down three things you are grateful for.
- Spend ten min drawing or doodling.
- Eat your meals without watching TV or using your cell phone.
- Start your morning with an affirmation.
- Decrease your social media time.
- Declutter your home, office, car.
- Light some candles, put on some music, and take a bubble bath.
- Do whatever makes you happy.

It doesn't matter if you do these things, but put forth an effort to start a plan of self-care.

6

OWN YOUR BEAUTY

Mirror, mirror on the wall, I believe in my beauty after all.

Living years without owning my beauty kept my self-esteem low. Most people would not believe that I have this problem. Inside is a terrified girl who only wants to be accepted for herself and not judged by her past. I held the key to unlocking the magical development of being myself. Only I had hidden it so deep that functioning behind a mask was my norm. I had not come to terms with my past, and this would make me feel like I wore a scarlet letter. The reflection from the mirror was distorted by my mindset. Constant evaluations of myself, trying to see what should be changed externally, not realizing it needed to come from within. The feeling of being unclean and nasty overshadowed my confidence. Every time I felt beautiful, the negative thoughts would immediately sabotage my outlook. It made me feel deserving of all the devastating experiences I went through. Although

The Mirror of Inner Beauty

I didn't discuss my pain, it showed up everywhere in my life and kept my self-esteem low.

I had no idea that I was projecting this negative behavior onto everything I wanted to achieve. Job promotions would come my way, but because of not truly believing in myself and my abilities, I got passed by. I needed to believe in myself, expect good things, and understand my worth. Self-hatred is a strong word to associate with yourself, and I wore it like a badge. Afraid to allow my light shine and be me.

Amazing how you can put on a mask just to survive. I have other alter egos besides Esther living in my head: Angela, AJ, and Angie. Me, myself, and I, for the most part. Angela and AJ are pretty much the same. AJ is a little more adventurous than Angela. Now Angie is the mean one. She only makes her presence known when she has finally had enough. All I can say is I hope you never have to encounter her because it will not be pretty.

Accepting a compliment was hard and awkward. My beauty was seen by others – I was the one who couldn't face the mirror. If someone said I was pretty, beautiful, kind, or just a great person, I downplayed it by giving an explanation as to why I wasn't worthy of such praise. A person's beauty, my beauty, to me, is defined by what someone has inside that illuminates to the outer shell. Its own energy takes your breath away or fills you with joy. Like a song that is beautifully written when sung by someone who can feel the words, it touches your soul and moves you.

One of my issues with how I look is with my hair. I have a love-hate relationship with my hair. It's soft and baby fine, so it doesn't hold curls very well and has never been long. Styling can be a chore. For many years I have worn wigs or hair extension to achieve what I thought made me beautiful. Holding on to feeling ugly because of my early trauma. Seeing my true beauty has helped with accepting those defeating feelings about myself. I know that who I am is not dependent on an accessory. My beauty comes from within, and regardless if my hair is slayed or looking like a hot mess, I'm still beautiful. Now with implementing self-care, I go and get my hair done every two weeks. It has become healthier and more manageable. There are still days that I wear wigs, but like I said, they are accessories and help to accentuate my inner beauty.

Early in 2018, I decided that I would take my desire to write a book seriously. I started researching and working with a close mentor on writing from my soul. An amazing opportunity came in the form of an author's workshop to develop the stories of our souls. When my mentor suggested I should attend, I didn't even blink. I paid my deposit and declared I was going. Then the worry set in. How in the hell was I going to pay for a plane ticket to Florida and a place to stay? Fortunately, my mentor and her roommate opened their home to me, and by having faith, I was able to have money for everything else. While attending this workshop, insecurities of feeling like I didn't

The Mirror of Inner Beauty

belong surfaced. No one made me feel that way, I just felt unworthy, as always.

We started a breathing exercise, and this is how I felt and came to my own self-realization about my beauty:

I'm uncomfortable; this is not a safe place for me. Why is he making me look deep inside myself? "Look in the mirror," he says. I don't want to; she is in the mirror. This was just supposed to be a breathing exercise. I don't like this, what if they see me? It's a mask I wear, like the wigs and makeup to cover up the awful, nasty, unclean part of me. No one knows who I am; if I take off the mask they will see. Oh God, help me, I'm uncomfortable. My eyes are closed, and the color purple appears like a majestic robe with green and gold sparkles. A key appears to open the door, but I'm terrified. The door opens, and inside is a mirror. The reflection is me, and to the side of my face is a mask. I'm beautiful; the mask is dark and ugly. My true inner self is beautiful. Breathe again deeper in thought; your abuse and mistakes don't make you ugly. You no longer need to have validation from others. No more hiding. Embrace your natural inner beauty.

After participating in this exercise, an intense feeling of relief overcame me, and tears began to fall. I finally understood that the outer layer is just a shell, and you can dress it up or down but the inner true self will shine like a bright light.

We were asked to take an hour away from the group to write down what we experienced and just let the feelings flow. I found this more difficult than participating in the exercise. Still setting limits on myself and overthinking. We were asked to share our writings with the group:

The purple, the green and gold covered the goddess, she is beautiful. The butterfly has emerged from her cocoon. The key opened the door. Her wings are beautiful; she can fly now. Be free, don't hide, no need to seek shelter anymore. Embrace your beauty. Others are in awe of it. You're not being arrogant or vain. You are just being you. See the beauty of the world all around. Live now and go forth. Speak and be heard, don't hesitate or hold back. You are absolutely amazing.

My journey to this realization has not been fun or easy, and the wounds are still healing. As I reflect on my life occurrences and now understand the damaging thoughts and patterns, I embrace the goddess that emerges within me.

Building my self-esteem was more than just accepting my reflection in the mirror. I needed to believe in myself and not just go through the motions. Daily affirmations, mantras, and inspirational thoughts wouldn't mean a thing if I didn't honestly believe them about myself. Blaming other people for my thoughts got me nowhere. The responsibility was mine alone.

The Mirror of Inner Beauty

Replaying arguments, discussions, and overthinking had me full of anxiety. Making me assume I didn't have the abilities to succeed.

I had a lot to be proud of, and for some reason, celebrating myself felt bad. Worse when the people in my circle weren't happy for my achievements. Many changes needed to be implemented, and the first step was believing that I had a purpose.

Reflecting Self-Esteem

I had no idea how deeply my trauma was affecting my self-esteem. I allowed the shame and guilt I felt from the abuse and promiscuous behavior to make me feel less than. I strived to be the best in everything I did but would immediately conform to not having enough confidence or value in myself. This would often keep me from being myself.

After experiencing this workshop, I began to feel differently about the reflection I saw in the mirror. I felt compassion and love for myself. I was no longer hiding behind a broken woman, but embracing the beautiful woman I am. I had to start seeing my worth and stop being afraid of the freedom it would bring.

I now want to wear makeup not to cover up any imperfection but to enhance what is already there; my beauty. I dress how I want to, not to impress or provoke a certain response but because I feel comfortable with myself. Learning to let go of the perfect person and enjoy the imperfect, unique qualities that make up me.

Instead of hiding, I'm shining my own light now and sharing my story to lead the way for others. My path continues to grow, and new opportunities keep presenting themselves. Fear shows up, Esther gets loud in my head, and then I start to get anxious. But then I remind myself this is not who you are anymore. Look in the mirror and see the beautiful spirit of yourself. That woman in the mirror is you, and she has potential and purpose.

The Mirror of Inner Beauty

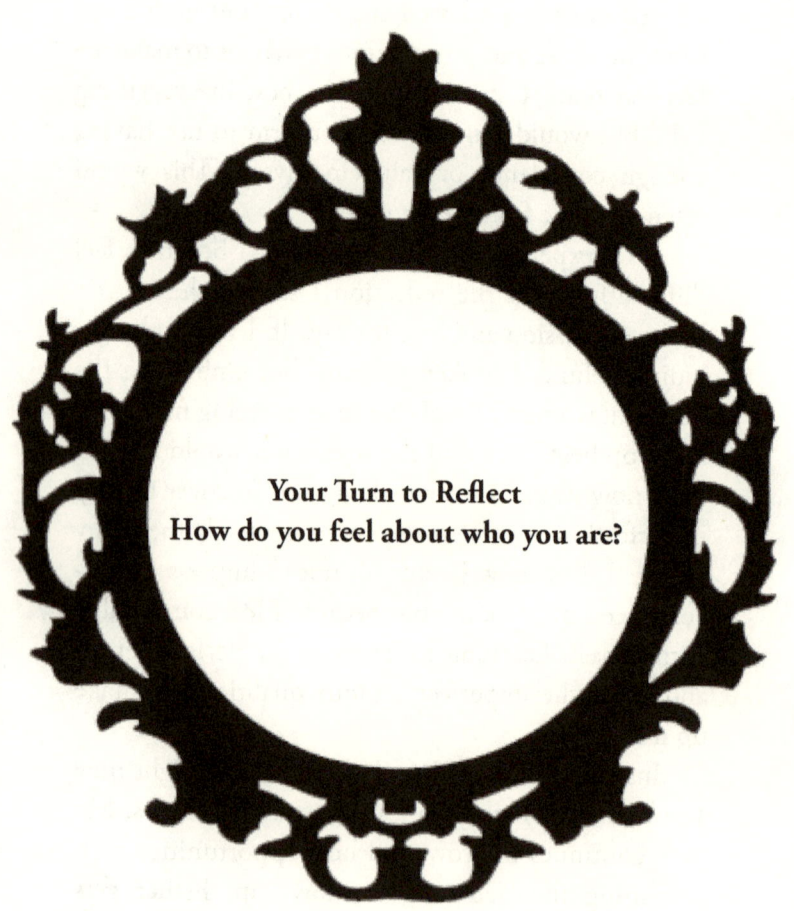

Your Turn to Reflect
How do you feel about who you are?

Angela Jones-Taul

They asked her, "How did you free yourself?"
She answered, "By embracing my own power."
- Yung Pueblo

7

MIRROR OF INNER BEAUTY

Mirror, mirror on the wall, I'm so glad I didn't fall. From that day of gloom and doom, to the goddess emerging with light and power, yes, it's me: the one I love and desired.

This chapter is the most important, to me. I can reflect on all my flaws and realize that somewhere between the innocence of childhood and adolescence, I lost love for myself. Buried it beneath the pain, ashamed of my scars and broken parts.

It was easy to pretend that I understood what self-love was, but that was a vague version. For me, I thought that just saying I loved myself was enough. Inside I didn't feel it or believe anyone could be capable of loving me. There was so much I needed to let go of and leave behind instead of picking it back up.

Most times when you express that you hate someone, you are ultimately stating that you no longer want them to exist. Your inner critic develops from early negative experiences in life. You then begin to develop your self-image around the negativity. Your expectations, the need to feel perfect, past trauma, and social comparison are all triggers that get your inner critic talking loudly inside your head. You may start to use negative statements about yourself, shy away from pursuing a dream, or feel uncomfortable being around others because of your thoughts. These thoughts and feelings start to consume you, and life becomes overwhelming. I strongly encourage anyone who may be experiencing the dark thoughts of ending your life or doing self-harm to seek counsel.

Learn to give yourself permission to feel. Then start exploring where these initial statements are coming from. Put value back into your life. Find the balance and stability within yourself. I searched for others to keep me grounded when all I needed was to find my true self and be okay with who I saw in the mirror and love her.

Noticing now that whenever a breakthrough is close, that's when I start to panic and want to run away, go back to being hidden and unseen. I fought hard to remain in my miserable codependent ways because it was safe. This was my insanity wanting to be this way, but my soul wanted to be more.

I never truly experienced having peace and calmness in my life until I began to love who I am. After the workshop, I decided that my story, this book, needed to be written. The company that held the workshop was sponsoring a book writing contest based on your soul story. I fretted about it and diminished my entry as not being good enough, but then I said to Esther, because she was the one doubting, "My story is important, and I have a chance, and that is all I need." I figured there was nothing to lose. Procrastinating until the last possible days to submit, I took a deep breath and hit the send button.

Waiting for the decision about who won the contest was less painful than dealing with my day-to-day routine. I was struggling with the amount of time and energy it took to run a business. My confidence in succeeding was diminishing. Comparing myself to others, wanting that instant gratification for my business to be successful and profitable. Unrealistic thinking, I had only been doing this full-time for nine months. "Cut yourself some slack, the lights are still on, and you are building up your clientele." These were the words I needed to tell myself to fight back the panic. "Live and stop trying to figure out what may or may not happen," another personal statement that would become a daily mantra.

September 21, 2018, would be the day that gave me a boost in believing in my purpose. I received two important phone calls that day. One was from two of the most amazing people placed on my path; they called to tell me I won the contest. I was in shock, and tears of joy flooded my face. When I got off the phone, I couldn't believe what just happened. My book is going to be written and published. I fell to my knees in gratitude and cried just a little more. Once I composed myself, I looked at my phone, and I had a voice message. "Congratulations, Angela Jones Taul, your business, Pure Touch Massage Center, was named Best of The Best for massage therapist in Maysville." I had to listen to the message again. When I returned the call, they repeated what I had just heard. I was waiting for someone to tell me this was all a mistake. There is no way I am having such a fabulous day, but it was all true.

Things started aligning for me. My clientele at my business began to grow, giving me a sense of accomplishment. The doubt and self-sabotaging behavior didn't serve me, but honoring myself did.

We have a testimony night twice a month at Celebrate Recovery. This is one of my favorite parts of the program. Finding the courage to speak about the experiences that shaped us. In April 2019, I gave my testimony in front of about 20 to 25 people in our large group session. This was the first time I would give an account of my hardships to a group. I was a nervous wreck. Practicing at home in front of a mirror I thought would help with the jitters and to share everything without tears. I was wrong; certain parts still triggered an emotional release. I would find out later from people in the audience that the raw emotion in my words touched them, even the males. Others were shocked and told me I hide my pain well. They would have never guessed I struggled with depression, anxiety, codependency, and low self-esteem.

A few days later, the pastor contacted me and asked if I would be willing to share my testimony at both services in a few weeks. Initially I was honored to be asked, but then worry started to set in. This would not be a small group to speak in front of. More like a few hundred at service, possibly another seventy-five to one hundred at the satellite site, and don't forget we stream online live. What would my haters say? More importantly, why was I worried about them? My story is important, someone may need to hear what I have to say. This was what I had to tell myself and Esther. Sunday morning came, and my stomach did flips. But I took a deep breath, walked out on stage, Kleenex in hand just in case, and give my testimony two more times.

The amount of love and support I felt was amazing. After the service, I was approached by so many people about how my story touched them or how it was relatable to theirs. The online streaming comments were just as supportive. My video has been viewed over 3,000 times. Wow, I never knew my story could have that type of impact.

I continued to grow in my Celebrate Recovery group. I lead a Step Study group, and at times give the message for the lesson. My journey keeps taking me further into what I believe is my purpose. To be a voice for women who have struggled in similar situations and be an inspiration. Who would have thought a recovery group could give me the much-needed freedom I desired in order to believe in my spirituality and allow it to serve as a tool for finding myself?

In June of 2019, I was able to attend The Summit of Hope for Celebrate Recovery. This was a three-day event and the most spiritually healing event I have attended in a long while. I felt exposed, opened, and free. Tears fell daily with each message, music, and just the overall experience. I honestly believe a deepened connection to my inner self emerged.

Here I am now writing my story, for the one person or multitude of people struggling with codependence, low self-esteem, self-hatred, body image issues, depression, or anxiety. Whatever the problem may be that is keeping you from experiencing your best life, you can release those old ways and start a new relationship with yourself.

Two of the biggest reasons I stay anxious and depressed are because I overthink situations and compare myself to others. I can take one situation and play out five different scenarios in my head. I can find fault within myself as to why I'm not as qualified as someone else is, even when we have the same education or opportunity. Setting expectations for others to understand my journey and validate me. This was unfair and didn't serve me. All it did was get me twisted in my head and spiral down into being the victim. I needed to believe that whatever was put on my heart to do was achieved by believing in myself. If I gave it my best and was committed, no other thought was needed.

My spiritual background is strong, and when I was lost in my faith, I walked in the dark more. I would withdraw and be reclusive. Attempting to control every outcome to all my problems. Anticipating something that may or may not happen and getting anxious. Putting the negative vibe out into the universe. When I just needed to incorporate some patience and faith. Be comfortable with attending church regularly and serving. Doing what I wanted, not what others dictated.

When I experienced days of only having the bare minimum to survive, I made it through. I still don't have all that I want, but I have what I need right now to get me to my next step. My insecurities became daily worries. Comparing my bad times against someone else's good fortune without knowing the whole story about what struggles they had. People often don't share the ugly, only the good. If you are like me, you pick apart your life based on half the story they presented.

We all have a choice in life, and sometimes that one decision may set us back or propel us to our next destination. Either way is a learning experience we must go through to move forward. I was asked to collaborate on a book with 11 other women when I was just finishing this one. I only knew a few of them from a mutual acquaintance, so I was nervous about contributing to this book. To be honest, I was burnt out from writing this story. Writing this story took me through hurt, healing, and happiness. I was in a wave of emotions and didn't want to start that all over again. When the co-publisher was helping me come up with a topic to write, she had suggested that I could use poetry.

This was like a green light for me to be myself; I feel like myself when I write poetry. It flows from me easily, no overthinking or feeling like I wouldn't measure up. They are my feelings and emotions, and no one can tell me how to feel about that. I submitted my part, and we now have a book out entitled *Women Standing Strong Together*. What an amazing, inspiring collection of stories from women of different backgrounds, standing strong and being vulnerable. Bringing hope and inspiration to others.

Wow, I was getting excited about my solo project, but this book is truly a gift for women. See what saying yes can bring you? Had I still been stuck in my comfort zone, allowing Esther to make the decision, I would have never taken the first step. Fear and doubt always show up to keep us from following our path, but once you trust in what has been placed on your heart, you can work through the stumbling blocks.

I now have two books to be proud of, and it all started with me wanting to become my authentic self. Not only did this journey bring me joy and happiness, it also has opened up opportunities for me to be a speaker at events. If you would have asked me years ago if I saw myself doing any of this, I would have looked at you like you were crazy. Yes, deep inside it was a desire and dream, but to live it out is an amazing feeling.

The Mirror of Inner Beauty

Once you start feeling comfortable with who you are, how you look, and what you have, your life starts to change. Old habits of "less than" will still surface when you come across someone who appears to have it all, but knowing that you are being the best version of you is all the validation you need.

Your process or steps may be different from mine, but making the effort to take care of yourself and realize that you have purpose will free you from the bondage of negativity. It's a glorious, exhilarating feeling that will take you deep inside yourself, and that is scary but so worth the risk to experience the greatest love of all, loving yourself.

The time is now for me to be everything I was placed on this earth to be. My scars and struggles were for a reason. Writing this book for my own healing and to help someone else heal is part of my purpose. The rest is yet to be determined.

Angela Jones-Taul

It takes a level of self-love, of dedication and determination to live your greatest life. So, look within. Look at every area of your life and ask yourself these questions: Am I on course? Am I growing mentally, emotionally and spiritually? Anything that is blocking that, anything that is preventing you from living your greatest life, make the tough decision to let it go. -Unknown

GODDESS MODE

I see myself as an emerging goddess, and during this transition, I began to evaluate the essence of my soul and what was important to me to focus on. Beauty, confidence, strength, love, gratitude, and happiness would be what I wanted to make stronger in my life. When the goddess made her appearance to me within my soul, I immediately felt I resonated with Aphrodite, the goddess of love and beauty. But after further investigation, I find that I'm Persephone. She is the goddess of spring and queen of the underworld. Her story has loss of innocence, grief, love, and celebration. Our stories have similarities from the early childhood trauma to finding the balance with the dark and light.

Once I began to adopt the goddess archetype, my focus words became important, and I took the time to define them in my own terms. When I honor my authentic self and release my goddess power to inspire, heal, and teach others, I experience the full Goddess Mode.

Goddess Mode
Total acceptance of the woman you are becoming. Knowing your worth and the unlimited capacity to make your life how you want it. Experiencing love, happiness, and joy on a whole new level. Emerge and rise, goddess.
– AJ

Angela Jones-Taul

Goddess Mode Beauty
The key to seeing your inner beauty is unlocking the false beliefs you placed on yourself. The natural ability to show compassion and encouragement. Our outer shell is an accessory. – AJ

Goddess Mode Confidence
Strong positive words, I am enough, and I am worthy, will build your confidence. Speak them daily. – AJ

Angela Jones-Taul

Goddess Mode Strength
Being and seeing youself at your best, letting go of yesterday, and starting a new day with hope and promise. – AJ

Goddess Mode Love
The deepest feeling of acceptance you can have for yourself. Commit to loving who you are. Be positive, kind, and patient with yourself. Accept every part of who you are unconditionally. – AJ

Angela Jones-Taul

Goddess Mode Gratitude
Being grateful daily will improve your self-being. You begin to focus on what you have and the good in your life. It opens you up to living happier. – AJ

The Mirror of Inner Beauty

Goddess Mode Happiness
The peaceful state of joy and love you have inside about yourself. My life is good. – AJ

My first love letter to myself dated 10/15/2017,
Dear Angela,

I love you. I know I don't tell you that enough, you probably don't think you deserve to hear it. You are kind and a good-hearted person. You didn't cause the wrongdoing that hurt you early in life. We will heal. I like the energy you generate when you smile. You bring joy to so many people, why not keep some of it for yourself? I like the version of you that laughs often because she is having fun. Stop looking for love; you hold the key to receiving the happiness you deserve. We are a work in progress. You are a self-sacrificing, empathetic person, all qualities to make you feel proud. Let's enjoy getting to know each other again – we lost some valuable time. I vow to always love you, no matter. You are worthy of being loved.

Love you,
Angela

STEPS FOR FINDING YOUR INNER GODDESS

There is no magic formula to free yourself from what may be keeping you from seeing your inner beauty. I want to offer some insight into some of the negative, self-critical things I struggled to acknowledge at first.

Find a group, recovery program, or therapist to talk through things. Never be ashamed of what you feel or have gone through. I suffered alone because it wasn't a normal practice to be open about the abuse.

Expectations
Setting high expectations and not meeting them can lead to feeling like you have failed. Our inner critic is very loud during these moments. Making us feel ashamed and disappointed in ourselves. This can be an overwhelming and difficult issue to live with, but there are steps to help quiet your inner critic.

The Mirror of Inner Beauty

What real expectations do you have for yourself?

Make an inventory list of your strengths. If this becomes hard, ask others to help you identify what they see. Examples: I'm compassionate, reliable, a good listener, passionate, independent.

1.
2.
3.
4.
5.
6.
7.
8.
9.
10.

Once you have your list, give yourself permission to accept these qualities.

Identifying the victim mentality
The victim mentality comes out of fear and a belief that your life is out of control. It's a coping mechanism that develops during the frustrations and demands of life. We adopt this behavior to avoid responsibility, get validation, and to feel we have a right to complain, making our environment toxic for ourselves and others.

My top ten signs of victim mentality:

1. Overreacting
2. Resistant to change
3. Self-criticism
4. Repeatedly sharing past tragedies Indiscriminately
5. Constantly comparing
6. Taking everything personally
7. Not living in gratitude
8. Extreme hopelessness
9. Inability to self-reflect
10. Frequent self-pity parties

Now that you have identified some traits, you can start to work on changing the behavior. Acknowledge that this is you and that you played a role in the choices you made. This is a hard step and may not be easy at first, but it's worth taking. You may feel this is another form of beating yourself up, but it's helpful.

The Mirror of Inner Beauty

Start asking yourself "why" and not "what." Cultivate a healthier belief system. When problems arise, immediately evaluate the situation. Don't react, but take it all in and then find the response. Always incorporate gratitude, and learn to celebrate yourself.

How do you answer compliments?
Do you accept them, or do you immediately put yourself down and minimize your worth? Example: "You look beautiful today." "No, I'm a hot mess," or "You can't be talking to me."

Practice just saying thank you, not adding a self-critical statement afterward.

Do you live in your past and revisit painful moments and emotions?
When we do this, we leave no room to forgive ourselves. Focus on what you have accomplished, no matter the time frame.

Give yourself a small goal to implement these changes, then take notes of the changed feeling you have toward yourself.

Set boundaries and start saying no. If you are unsure about committing to something, ask for time to think about it, give yourself time to make sure it's the right decision for you.

Find a support system to keep you uplifted and focused. Sometimes your support will come from those who aren't family or close friends. You must find the strength to believe in yourself and your dreams.

Allow others to have their own opinions and feelings. Don't put unnecessary pressure on yourself. Opportunities come, and if we allow our fears to take over, we miss out on a chance to experience our life to the fullest. No one wants to always wonder or play the what-if game. Just imagine if you plugged in the positive outcomes instead of the negative ones.

How does that change your outlook on decision making?

We sometimes find it hard to look at ourselves with gratitude. Instead we see judgment. Start a list of daily affirmations, place them next to your mirror, and recite them in your daily routine. Here are a few that help reverse the negative reflection you might have for yourself:

I am Enough
I am Loved
I am Amazing
I am Not My Mistakes

I am Worthy
I am Beautiful
I am Unique

The Mirror of Inner Beauty

Fear shows up in life more times than we care to admit. It paralyzes and keeps us from moving forward. Learning to conquer fear isn't a quick and easy fix. It takes time and the desire to want change. I still have times when I allow fear to control my progress. The good news is I have learned to pinpoint those unhealthy coping mechanisms I cling to when fear shows up. Here is a list of them:

1. Worrying
2. Procrastinating
3. Comparing myself to others
4. Emotional eating
5. Blaming others

My positive coping mechanisms to counteract the negative ones:

1. Live in gratitude
2. Let go of fear, and make a plan
3. Stop it
4. Find something constructive to do, remind myself I'm not hungry
5. Self-reflect and take responsibility

List your unhealthy coping mechanisms, then positive ways to counteract.

The Mirror of Inner Beauty

Fear has been spelled out in many acronym sayings. Find one that fits your life and situation and post it somewhere you will see it daily. Mine is at my desk at my business.

False	**F**orget
Evidence/Emotions	**E**verything
Appearing	**A**nd
Real	**R**un

Now turn those to positive affirmations

Face	**F**ocus
Everything	**E**quip
And	**A**ct
Rise	**R**elease

Self-Sabotage and Comparing

These two subjects I feel kept me blocked and still cause me to stumble at times.

Self-sabotaging is knowing what needs to be done to improve, but procrastinating or feeling you need to wait until the perfect time, or staying in the comfort zone. You feel the tug to take the leap but talk yourself out of it because "what if."

Steps to reverse self-sabotaging behavior:

1. Identify the behavior and pinpoint the triggers. Pinpoint your pattern; do you overthink a situation? What are you afraid of really?
2. Recommit to goals.
3. Monitor your negative thoughts.
4. Celebrate you.

The Mirror of Inner Beauty

Comparing yourself to others is such an unfair, unfulfilling process that will keep you stuck. Everyone starts at a different place and has different situations. You may never know how much time and effort they had to put into their project or endeavors by just looking from the outside.

Steps to stop comparing:

1) Focus on yourself.
2) Accept where you are in your life and take steps to get where you want to be.
3) Take a vacation from social media.
4) Live in gratitude.
5) Find inspiration and learn from others.
6) Compare only with yourself.

Attitude of Gratitude:

1. Keep a daily gratitude list
2. Make a reflective inventory list. Include what your triggers were and how you dealt with them.
3. Do a bedtime brain dump to clear your mind for a restful night.
4. Meditate

Angela Jones-Taul

Whispers from An Angel

When I was born an angel whispered to me
The essence of your soul is locked with a key
You hold the access deep within and you won't immediately see
What your light is meant to be.

As my light began to shine within
The world would introduce me to sin
A loss of innocence and burdened with shame
My light became dim and I took the blame.

Too much for my young mind to bear
I became lost, feeling like no one cared
The dark shadows are what appealed to me now
My inner voice Esther would reign with her crown
Spent years developing a mask that could hide
The raging battle going on in my mind.

Once again, my angel whispered in my ear
Keep shining your light and dry up those tears
I felt a wave of redeeming grace
Knowing this wasn't the end of my race.

The Mirror of Inner Beauty

My light began to brighten my soul
The darkness would fight to gain control
This time it would deliver a devastating blow
To punish my growth and dim my glow.

I wanted to end this torturous game
I attempted to extinguish my beautiful flame
My angel would appear once again
Not to whisper but to proclaim
If you don't own your gifts from within
I have no choice but to let the darkness win
Ignite your flame and shine it bright
Your inner beauty has always been the light.

Balance your light with the dark
Embracing Esther is where you start
Give her love and she will see
That your purpose will bring you peace.

Angela Jones-Taul

No longer relating to the negative words
Unworthy, unloved and even unclean
Shed your mask and add some vulnerability
You have a new name to claim and positive energy

Let's start with loved, worthy and enough
Add courageous and independent, girl strut your stuff
I love who I am, this is me
An emerging goddess
So it is, So it be.

My angel came once again and whispered to me
You've always had purpose
I just needed you to see
What an amazing woman you turned out to be.

Potential and Purpose

Potential and purpose dwells in my soul
My goddess colors purple, green and glorious gold
An empowered woman who will help fix your crown
'Cause potential and purpose is what I found

No longer denying but accepting my worth
Please honor my rebirth
Love, beauty, confidence in check
Full goddess mode in effect

Motivating and inspiration are my goals
For all women sparkle, some just don't know
They have potential and purpose hidden deep within
Positive encouragement will help them win

I build my tribe with powerful women
The ones whose hearts are full of giving
Role models to all with their service
All women have potential and purpose

Our outreach is for the young and seasoned
This is from our heart, no other reason
Women coming together as one
Potential and purpose have begun.

About the Author

After suffering abuse at an early age, Angela Jones spiraled into a life of self-loathing and shame, hiding behind a mask and feeling she didn't deserve love or acceptance. But through a series of life-altering events and realizations, Angela transitioned from victim to victor. Take this journey with Angela and you just might gather the courage to strip off *your* mask, look into "The Mirror of Inner Beauty," and illuminate the true essence of your soul.

Angela Jones Taul is an author, LPN, Licensed Massage Therapist, energy healer, mentor and inspirational speaker. She is the owner of Pure Touch Massage Center in Maysville Ky. Angela a contributing author to the best seller Women Standing Strong Together. An active participant in her church community, Angela leads a women's open share and step study group for the Celebrate Recovery Ministry. She is currently working on her yoga teacher certification and plans to integrate yoga with the recovery program. Resonating with a goddess mentality helped her to find the strength to let her light shine. In her free time, she enjoys being a grandmother and writing poetry. You can reach her at angelashines@yahoo.com and https://angelashines.wixsite.com/website.

www.ingramcontent.com/pod-product-compliance
Lightning Source LLC
LaVergne TN
LVHW041337080426
835512LV00006B/508